AMERICAN POLICY TOWARD
COMMUNIST EASTERN EUROPE

AMERICAN POLICY TOWARD COMMUNIST EASTERN EUROPE: THE CHOICES AHEAD

BY JOHN C. CAMPBELL

THE UNIVERSITY OF MINNESOTA PRESS
Minneapolis

Library of Congress Catalog Card Number: 65-15982

PUBLISHED IN GREAT BRITAIN, INDIA, AND PAKISTAN BY THE OXFORD
UNIVERSITY PRESS, LONDON, BOMBAY, AND KARACHI, AND IN CANADA
BY THE COPP CLARK PUBLISHING CO. LIMITED, TORONTO

PREFACE

Twenty-five years ago, a hundred million people living in the countries between Germany and Russia were cut off from normal contact with the rest of the world. After the Second World War, instead of regaining their freedom, they were absorbed into the Russian Communist empire. For years America regarded the entire region as part of a monolithic Communist bloc, but now important changes are taking place. Resurgent nationalism, changes in the Soviet Union, and the Sino-Soviet split have shaken the Communist bloc. Viewing these events, Americans have begun to ask questions about our relations with the individual states of Communist Eastern Europe.

This volume traces the history of United States relations with the area and gives factual background about the military, political, economic, and psychological aspects of our policy. In identifying the main policy issues that confront the United States it describes a number of alternative courses that this nation might pursue. Through the problem approach it helps the reader to understand and come to grips with the range of possible actions and to reach his own conclusions on the course most appropriate for the United States.

This paper, now in book form, was originally prepared to serve as the basis for discussion at the Seventh Midwest Seminar on United States Foreign Policy, held May 13–16, 1964, at Wingspread, The Johnson Foundation National Conference Center at Racine, Wisconsin. The paper was prepared at the request of the Committee by Dr. John C. Campbell. It does not necessarily reflect the views of the Committee or any of its members or staff.

Dr. Campbell is well known as an expert on Eastern European and Middle Eastern affairs. He served in the State Department for a number of years, as Specialist in Eastern Europe, Officer in Charge of Balkan Affairs, Deputy Director of the Office of East European Affairs, and member of the Policy Planning Staff. He is the author of *Defense of the Middle East,* three volumes of *The United States in World Affairs,* and numerous articles on foreign relations. He is now Senior Research Fellow of the Council on Foreign Relations.

The Seminar is a joint effort of the Universities of Illinois, Indiana, Michigan, Minnesota, and Wisconsin, and is the latest in a series of programs dating back to 1952. Since the Seventh Seminar the University of Iowa has joined the Committee. The University of Minnesota was the host institution for the 1964 Seminar. The Seminar was financed by a grant from The Johnson Foundation. This grant reflects the continuing interest of The Foundation and its officers in broadening public understanding of key issues in the contemporary world.

The Seminar was prepared under the direction of the Midwest University Committee. Associated with the Committee in the presentation of this and previous seminars has been The Brookings Institution of Washington. H. Field Haviland, Director of the Foreign Policy Studies Division of Brookings, has provided the Committee with continuing assistance and support. In its work the Committee has profited from the continuing personal interest and support of Leslie Paffrath, President of The Johnson Foundation.

> William C. Rogers, *1964 Chairman*
> *Midwest University Committee*

UNIVERSITY OF ILLINOIS: Royden J. Dangerfield
UNIVERSITY OF INDIANA: Edward H. Buehrig
UNIVERSITY OF IOWA: Vernon Van Dyke
UNIVERSITY OF MICHIGAN: Henry L. Bretton
UNIVERSITY OF MINNESOTA: William C. Rogers
UNIVERSITY OF WISCONSIN: James R. Donoghue

AUTHOR'S NOTE

THIS book, first written in the form of a background paper for a conference of distinguished private citizens and government officials, is intended to perform that same service for groups and individuals all over the country, in universities, public forums, and elsewhere — wherever there is interest in American foreign policy. It is, essentially, a problem paper presenting information and analysis on which judgments can be based and setting forth alternative policies open to the United States in regard to Eastern Europe. I have not attempted to argue a case or to give my own conclusions on policy. The purpose is to stimulate intelligent discussion of the important issues at stake.

Two of the chapters were originally published elsewhere: the analysis of recent political trends in Eastern Europe (Chapter II) by the House Committee on Foreign Affairs (*Recent Developments in the Soviet Bloc*, Hearings before the Subcommittee on Europe, Part II, Washington: Government Printing Office, 1964), and the study of Yugoslavia (Chapter V) as an article in *Foreign Affairs* (January 1963), which has given permission for its use. Both have been revised for the present publication.

I should like to express thanks to Professor William C. Rogers, Chairman of the Seventh Midwest Seminar, for continuing and wise counsel; to Mr. Leslie Paffrath, President of The Johnson Foundation; and to all who participated in the discussion at Wingspread. A special word of appreciation is due Miss Helen Caruso, who helped with the manuscript and prepared the index.

FACTS AND FIGURES

Albania
OFFICIAL NAME: People's Republic of Albania
CAPITAL: Tirana
AREA: 11,096 square miles
POPULATION: 1,736,000
PRINCIPAL LEADERS:
> President of the Presidium: Haxhi Lleshi
> Premier: Mehmet Shehu
> First Secretary of the Albanian Labor Party: Enver Hoxha

Bulgaria
OFFICIAL NAME: People's Republic of Bulgaria
CAPITAL: Sofia
AREA: 42,729 square miles
POPULATION: 8,045,200
PRINCIPAL LEADERS:
> Chief of State, President of the Presidium of the National Assembly: Georgi Traikov
> Premier: Todor Zhivkov
> First Secretary of the Central Committee of the Bulgarian Communist Party: Todor Zhivkov

Czechoslovakia
OFFICIAL NAME: Czechoslovak Socialist Republic
CAPITAL: Prague
AREA: 49,366 square miles
POPULATION: 13,981,000

PRINCIPAL LEADERS:
>President: Antonín Novotný
>Premier: Jozef Lenárt
>First Secretary of the Communist Party of Czechoslovakia: Antonín Novotný

Hungary

OFFICIAL NAME: Hungarian People's Republic
CAPITAL: Budapest
AREA: 35,912 square miles
POPULATION: 10,091,000
PRINCIPAL LEADERS:
>President of the Praesidium: István Dobi
>Chairman of the Council of Ministers: János Kádár
>First Secretary of the Hungarian Socialist Workers' Party: János Kádár

Poland

OFFICIAL NAME: Polish People's Republic
CAPITAL: Warsaw
AREA: 120,359 square miles
POPULATION: 30,690,000
PRINCIPAL LEADERS:
>Chairman of the Council of State: Edward Ochab
>Premier: Jozef Cyrankiewicz
>First Secretary of the Polish United Workers' Party: Wladyslaw Gomulka

Rumania

OFFICIAL NAME: Rumanian People's Republic
CAPITAL: Bucharest
AREA: 91,699 square miles
POPULATION: 19,000,000
PRINCIPAL LEADERS:
>President of the State Council: Chivu Stoica
>Premier: Ion Gheorghe Maurer
>First Secretary of the Rumanian Workers' Party: Nicolae Ceausescu

Yugoslavia

OFFICIAL NAME: Socialist Federal Republic of Yugoslavia
CAPITAL: Belgrade

AREA: 98,674 square miles
POPULATION: 18,841,000
PRINCIPAL LEADERS:
    President: Josip Broz-Tito
    Vice President: Aleksandar Ranković
    President of the Federal Assembly: Edvard Kardelj
    Secretary General of the League of Communists of Yu-
        goslavia: Josip Broz-Tito

TABLE OF CONTENTS

AMERICAN POLICY TOWARD
COMMUNIST EASTERN EUROPE

I *HISTORICAL BACKGROUND*

THE fate of the captive nations of Eastern Europe has been an important concern of American foreign policy ever since those nations came under the sway of the Soviet Union in the aftermath of the Second World War. It has also been something of a football of American domestic politics, kicked most vigorously at four-year intervals when presidential elections occur. For many years, regardless of the volume of American oratory, the lines of the cold war were so rigidly drawn that there was little we could do about Eastern Europe. More recently, changes within the Soviet empire itself, some of them sparked by the split between Moscow and Peking, have brought new, though still limited, opportunities for Western statesmanship. Above all, they have given the United States greater possibilities of choice. They have put Eastern Europe in a position where decisions concerning it are pertinent to the main directions of American foreign policy.

In the past few years Presidents John F. Kennedy and Lyndon Johnson have espoused a policy of treating Communist countries in different ways according to their different circumstances, of "building bridges" to Eastern Europe, and of seeking areas of agreement with the Soviet Union while maintaining necessary defense strength. President Johnson's decisive electoral victory over Senator Barry Goldwater in November 1964 followed a campaign in which the latter directly challenged that policy and urged a broad offensive aimed at victory over Communism. It is impossible to say to what extent the vote of the American people turned on

3

that particular issue. In any case, it will surely continue to be debated, and the question of precisely what should be done concerning Eastern Europe remains before the administration, the Congress, and the people.

The terms in which that question must be answered will not remain static. They will depend in many ways on decisions taken outside this country: in Moscow and the capitals of Eastern Europe, as well as in Western Europe and in Peking. The fall from power of Nikita Khrushchev and the uncertainty over the directions in which his successors will push, or be pushed, point in striking fashion to the wide gaps always present in any assessment of Soviet policy we may make. One has only to think back to the unexpected consequences of Stalin's passing from the seat of power some twelve years ago. Yet uncertainty does not justify a retreat from thought or from action. There is all the more reason to look carefully at the background of the problem before us, and especially at those elements of it likely to transcend the comings and goings of individual actors on the stage.

The Troubled Past of a Borderland

Historically, Eastern Europe — the nations between Germany and Austria on one side and Russia and Turkey on the other, and from the Baltic to the Black, Aegean, and Adriatic seas — has been a borderland of empires and a battleground between them. Its peoples have been objects rather than subjects in the great sweep of history. Yet in this amorphous region have lain many points of contention affecting the balance of power in Europe and the peace of the world.

Over the centuries the nations of Eastern Europe — Baltic peoples, Poles, Czechs and Slovaks, Hungarians, Rumanians, Croats and Serbs, Bulgarians, Albanians, Greeks — did not develop strong and enduring state structures or firm political institutions, although each at one time or another enjoyed a period of glory which later became a symbol and stimulus to nationalist aspirations. Weakness was due in no small part to fragmentation and diversity, for in contrast to the West the ethnic map of Eastern Europe became a patchwork quilt of nationalities and linguistic groups. They lived submerged, without strong leaders of their own, or enjoyed a precarious autonomy or fleeting independence on the fringes of great empires.

When the age of nationalism arrived, and leaders of the awakening in each nation translated ethnic differences into political and territorial demands, the stage was set for a series of struggles against neighboring empires and among the nations of Eastern Europe themselves. Nationalism did not remedy the basic fact of weakness in relation to outside powers, for whom the area continued to be one of contention, but added to it through the intensity of the internal conflicts which set the various nationalities against one another. During the nineteenth century most of the Balkan nations won their independence from the Ottoman empire, generally with the support of great powers; although those changes were acts of historic justice, the main result was to replace the weakness and uncertainties of the rule of Europe's "sick man," as Turkey was known, with the sharper conflicts and more explosive potentialities of their own. With the First World War came the turn of the Baltic nations, Poland, and the peoples of the Hapsburg empire.

The peace settlement following the First World War marked a great triumph of nationalism, thanks partly to Woodrow Wilson and the policies of the United States. With some notable exceptions, the new frontiers in Eastern Europe were drawn in accordance with the principle of nationalities and the Fourteen Points. But the repudiation of the peace settlement and of the League of Nations by the United States left all the countries of that region with only partial assurance of the outside support they were bound to need in the future.

The Second World War

Between the two world wars Eastern Europe remained the scene of disputes over frontiers and national minorities that helped to prevent any consolidation of the peace. The states were too small to stand on their own and too antagonistic to work together.

The alliances of the period merely intensified the gulf between the *status quo* group (Poland, Czechoslovakia, Yugoslavia, Rumania, Greece) generally supported by France, and the revisionist states (Hungary, Bulgaria, Albania) generally supported by Germany and Italy. The French alliance network and the collective security system of the League of Nations did not survive the pressures put upon them. The depression of the 1930s and the weakness of the Western democracies forced most of the Eastern European states to turn to Germany; only after Munich (1938) did the British finally decide to make a stand with their guarantee to Poland in 1939, a step which made sure that the Second World War, when it came, would have its immediate cause in Eastern Europe. Perhaps Poland was more a symbol of the need to stop Hitler somewhere than a vital Western interest, but the fact remained that it was in Eastern Europe that the existing world balance was challenged and there that the challenge was answered. Although the Western nations could not save Poland from Hitler, with his attack the struggle was joined and the fate of all the nations of Europe was in the crucible of war.

Actually, the fate of Eastern Europe depended more on its geographical position between Germany and Russia than on what the West might do. In the interwar period its nations had enjoyed an artificial and temporary serenity because the power of both neighboring giants had been smashed in the first war. As both recovered and gained in strength, it depended largely on them whether the territory in between was fought over, left alone, or partitioned into spheres of influence. The Eastern European states could only seek whatever shelter they could get by making agreements with one or the other of the two predators or by looking to the West for help. The Hitler-Stalin agreements of August and September 1939 had the effect of dividing the area between them, but the status of some countries, particularly Bulgaria, remained obscure. Here lay the seeds of misunderstanding and dispute from which grew Hitler's attack on Russia in June 1941.

Germany attacked and overran Yugoslavia and Greece in April 1941. Soon after, with Germany's rapid military success on the

Russian front, all of Eastern Europe came under German domination. For the next four years the map showed some strange configurations, with former states like Poland, Czechoslovakia, and Yugoslavia erased altogether, new ones such as Slovakia and Croatia enjoying a shadow independence under ultimate German dominance, and other areas under varying degrees of military occupation and control. Those which had chosen not to resist (Hungary, Rumania, Bulgaria) became satellites, allowed to retain their own governments as long as they cooperated in the German war effort.

The Communist Takeover

Giving no recognition to the wartime changes brought about by the Germans and Italians and their quislings in Eastern Europe, the United States continued to recognize the governments-in-exile of Poland, Czechoslovakia, Yugoslavia, and Greece. President Roosevelt and Prime Minister Churchill proclaimed in the Atlantic Charter (1941) their desire to see no territorial changes that did not accord with the freely expressed will of the peoples concerned, and their respect for the right of all peoples to choose the form of government under which they will live. These principles were reiterated in solemn pledges signed also by Stalin,[1] but the critical questions were decided not by declarations but by the fortunes of war and the facts of geography. Eastern Europe, except Greece, fell within the theater of operations of the Soviet armies. Where those armies marched, political power sooner or later came into the hands of the Communists. In two states where they appeared only briefly or not at all, Yugoslavia and Albania, the local Communist movement had enough military force and political strength to win and hold power by itself.

The Baltic states (Estonia, Latvia, Lithuania) were reincorporated in the Soviet Union as soon as they were reconquered. The base of the new government in Poland was a Communist group installed by the Soviet Union. Moscow, despite its own agreements to the contrary, fended off and frustrated all efforts of the Western

[1] See the text of the Declaration on Liberated Europe (Appendix A).

powers to broaden the provisional government by including fair representation for democratic parties and to ensure a free election. In Rumania the Soviet Union by its own fiat put in power a Communist-dominated regime and helped to keep it there despite Western protests. In Bulgaria it backed the local Communists in their seizure of power and destruction of all rivals. In Hungary the process was somewhat slower; a free election was even permitted in 1945, but though the Communists were badly defeated they stayed in the coalition government and eventually destroyed it. Nowhere else in Eastern Europe, except in Czechoslovakia in 1946, did free elections take place, despite solemn pledges to hold them. Nowhere, we may be quite sure, would the Communists have won anything like a majority.

For tactical reasons the Soviets made haste slowly, once they had made sure that the local Communists would have the leading role in the new postwar governments and that the "bourgeois" elements were under control. They could have attempted immediately to establish full-blown Communist dictatorships but chose instead to maintain coalitions, or the appearance of coalitions, for a period during which the Communists were entrenching themselves in the police and security apparatus, the courts, the local administration, labor unions, and the means of communication. Generally they took care to have in their own hands the key ministries of interior, finance, justice, and propaganda. In disposing of non-Communist parties they weakened them by forming rival splinter groups and eventually sliced them off the body politic one by one, using what the Hungarian Communist leader Mátyás Rákosi termed "salami tactics." In almost every country the Socialist parties were forced into amalgamation with the Communists in a "united workers' party." Opposition leaders were persecuted, driven into exile, and in some cases seized, tried, and sentenced to death or long imprisonment. With the final elimination of all real opposition, the Eastern European states emerged as "people's democracies" under the control and direction of one party, the Communist. The form of government, again to quote

Rákosi, was the "dictatorship of the proletariat but not in the Soviet form."

The process did not go uniformly in tactic or in tempo throughout Eastern Europe though the general pattern was the same. In Bulgaria, Rumania, and Hungary the Soviet authorities were supposedly acting under the terms of armistice agreements concluded jointly by the three major allied powers with those former German satellites. Although the British and American representatives who sat on the Allied Control Commissions were generally ignored by the Soviet commanders, whose superior position rested on the fact of Soviet military occupation, their presence served as a momentary check on the speed of the takeover. But in the end neither the armistice agreements nor the pledges of free elections were honored. The Western powers could do nothing to save those political leaders who were their friends (except the few they helped to escape). Communist control was well established in Bulgaria as early as 1944, in Rumania in 1945, and in Hungary two years later, although its opponents did not give up their resistance.

Meanwhile, peace treaties with the three countries had been concluded and were signed in February 1947. They contained broad obligations to protect human rights, but they were no more effective in practice than the armistice agreements or the declarations of Yalta. Soviet forces evacuated Bulgaria in 1947 when the treaties came into force; they stayed in Rumania and Hungary, ostensibly to protect the line of communication to the Soviet occupation forces in Austria. Their real purpose in the two latter countries, where the Communists were an unpopular minority, was to keep things in line and to leave the people in no doubt where ultimate power resided.

Poland was in many ways the test case. Britain had gone to war on the issue of Poland's independence. The United States, partly because of its own large number of citizens of Polish descent, was especially desirous of seeing the Poles free to choose their own government. Stalin, on the other hand, would be satisfied only with a Poland that would be "friendly" to the Soviet Union, which as he interpreted it meant a Poland under Soviet and Communist control. Through all the negotiations and compromises with the Western powers, which played so prominent a part in East-West relations during and after the war, he stuck to his purpose and he was successful. The "provisional government" formed as a result of agreement at Yalta, though enlarged to include Stanislaw Mikolajczyk, former premier of the government-in-exile, and other non-Communists, remained essentially an instrument of the Communists, and the campaign for the election of a new government was nothing but a travesty of fair play. The election itself, held in January 1947, was conducted under Communist control and had the expected outcome. In the following years the Communist grip steadily closed tighter on the country.

Czechoslovakia followed a separate course. Its wartime government-in-exile was the only such government able to return to Eastern Europe, because its head, President Eduard Beneš, took the step of reaching prior agreement with Stalin against the advice of his Western allies. This deliberate policy of working with and depending on the Soviet Union made it virtually certain that the local Communists would play a leading role in postwar Czechoslovakia and that the country's foreign policies would be acceptable to Moscow. In the election of 1946, which was free, the Communists got 38 per cent of the vote, the largest total of any party. Their leader, Klement Gottwald, became prime minister of a coalition government in which the key ministry of internal affairs was also in Communist hands. The means were there to organize "action committees" and other instruments for the seizure of full power when the time should become ripe for it.

Beneš hoped that the Czech Communists would work with other parties in the democratic tradition of the prewar republic. He and his foreign minister, Jan Masaryk, hoped that Czechoslovakia could retain some independence in foreign policy and serve as a bridge between East and West while taking care to conform generally to the Soviet line. He proved wrong on both counts. Stalin's veto of Czechoslovakia's decision to participate in the Marshall Plan demonstrated beyond doubt that there could be no independent foreign policy. The internal crisis that came to a head in February 1948 confirmed that the Communists scorned democratic procedures and that the only alternative to handing over power to them lay in a trial by arms. Beneš was not willing to make the choice for civil war and therefore gave way. The presence of Soviet troops on the frontier, ready to march in to support the Communists, was one of the determining factors in his choice.

1948: The Meaning of Tito's Break

The year of the Communist seizure of power in Czechoslovakia, which appeared to complete the Soviet domination of Eastern Europe, was also the year of the first crack in the monolith: the assertion of independence by Tito's Yugoslavia. Late in 1947 the Communist parties of the Soviet Union, of the Eastern European satellites, and of France and Italy had met to found the Information Bureau, or Cominform, which was to coordinate their activities. Its seat was to be Belgrade, a fitting recognition of the prestige the Yugoslav Communists had won as the most successful builders of socialism outside the Soviet Union — and presumably the most loyal followers of Stalin. Tito seemed to be "the eldest son of the Church." But appearances were deceptive.

The Yugoslav Communist leaders had won power in their country through their own strength and organization. Tito, though he was an old Comintern agent, governed Yugoslavia because he and his partisans had won a civil war, and they did not owe their position to Moscow's help. He sought cooperation with the Soviet party but was not its puppet. He had his own army and police system. He even had, within the Communist bloc, his own foreign policy, evident in his differences with Moscow on the questions of Balkan federation and of the Greek civil war. When Stalin, to make sure of his own ultimate control, attempted to infiltrate his own agents into that army and police system, he met resistance. When he tried to insist on the kind of unequal political and economic arrangements by which he dominated the other Eastern European states, the Yugoslavs said no. Then came the thunderous denunciation of Tito, the Cominform Resolution of June 28, 1948.

Tito was accused of various doctrinal sins and deviations. But the real differences were not over doctrine. They were over political power, over who was to control Yugoslavia. Tito had that control and he would not give it up. Himself an old hand at the Communist techniques of seizing and holding power, he was far more effective than a Mikolajczyk or a Beneš in maintaining his positions. He did not want the quarrel with Stalin, but he stood his ground when Stalin threatened the base of his power and called on "loyal" Communists to overthrow him. When Stalin pursued that line by all means short of armed attack, Tito was driven into a position of defiance. He was as tough with Cominformists in Yugoslavia as he had been with his bourgeois opponents.

Having been read out of the international Communist movement and subjected to military threats and other severe pressures, Tito and his colleagues took every opportunity of getting support, including military and economic aid from the West, for the defense of Yugoslavia's independence. Their treaties of alliance with the Soviet bloc having been broken, they looked to the United Nations and improved relations with their free-world neighbors (Austria, Italy, and Greece); they joined in a Balkan pact with Greece and Turkey, two members of NATO, but shied away from any more direct tie with NATO.

Under attack from Stalin, Tito counterattacked with a vigorous propaganda campaign against him and his regime. The main theme was that it was Stalin who had departed from Marxism-Leninism to establish a bureaucratic despotism, while Yugoslavia had held to the correct way. That theme might not have much effect in the Soviet Union itself, but it had disruptive possibilities in the Soviet satellite states of Eastern Europe. Not that the peoples of those countries had any reason to regard Tito with any hope; his was still a tight and ruthless Communist dictatorship scarcely different from that of their own Stalinist regimes. His appeal was directed primarily to Communist leaders and functionaries who might be restive under Soviet direction, especially those who had a local rather than a "Muscovite" background. The salient point was not Yugoslavia's theories of Marxism but the fact of its independence *as a Communist state*. Had Yugoslavia become bourgeois or fascist, as Stalin declared it had, it would not incite the envy of Eastern European Communists. But Tito, though he followed an independent foreign policy and had no hesitation in improving relations with the Western powers and asking them for support, made no retreat at all from his stance as a believing Communist building socialism in his country.

Stalin saw the danger and met it in his usual ruthless style. He ordered purges in the satellite parties of all Titoists and potential Titoists. Many prominent Communist leaders were arrested and condemned in rigged show-trials. The luckier ones were imprisoned; others were executed. Among those removed from the political scene were Gomulka in Poland, Rajk and Kádár in Hungary, Kostov in Bulgaria, Patrascanu and Pauker in Rumania, Xoxe in Albania, Slánský and Clementis in Czechoslovakia. The accompanying reign of terror, with power tightly held in the hands of Stalin's trusted proconsuls, disposed of any possible challenge.

The terror continued to be visited upon the non-Communist majorities as well as upon its many victims within the respective Communist parties. These were the years of the full consolidation of Communist power in Eastern Europe under Stalin's direction and control. All nuclei of possible opposition were destroyed. Constitutions modeled on that of the Soviet Union were adopted. The old middle class was driven out of all remaining positions of any significance in the professions or the economy. The collectivization drive against the independent peasantry was pushed hard. The industrial workers, the supposed leaders and beneficiaries of the Communist revolution, were exploited like everyone else, caught up in the feverish drive for forced-draft industrialization. Throughout Eastern Europe — outside heretical Yugoslavia — there was total fear, and total Soviet supremacy.[2]

[2] The imposition of the Stalinist system on Eastern Europe is described in detail in Stephen D. Kertesz (ed.), *The Fate of East Central Europe: Hopes and Failures of American Policy* (Notre Dame, Ind.: University of Notre Dame Press, 1956). Excerpts from Professor Kertesz's introductory chapters to this and to the volume that succeeded it, *East Central Europe and the*

The Thaw

Stalin's system in the satellites, as in the Soviet Union, seemed impregnable, but things that began to happen soon after his death proved that it was not. Whether it was his disappearance that brought the change or whether it had to come anyway, the fact is that Communist Eastern Europe entered a new period in 1953. Some of the pressures that had been accumulating began to break through the discipline of the system. Riots in East Germany and in Czechoslovakia gave evidence of the intensity of popular discontent. The new rulers of the Soviet Union, though they did not hesitate to use force to restore order in East Germany, found that it was anything but easy to run an empire without an emperor. And so, in many ways and for many reasons — uncertainty over satellite leadership and its ability to control the subject peoples, the need for decompression in Eastern Europe as well as in the Soviet Union, the obvious failure of many Stalinist economic policies, and some slackening of party discipline and police terror — the ties that bound the satellite capitals rigidly to Moscow were loosened.

Khrushchev's abandonment of the feud with Tito in 1955 and the new line he took at the Twentieth Congress of the Soviet Communist Party in 1956 had the effect of endorsing Tito's theory of separate roads to socialism. Quite naturally these events gave vast encouragement to elements in the Communist parties of Eastern Europe which were already showing signs of restiveness with what was still an essentially Stalinist system. Especially among the intellectuals — writers, poets, journalists, teachers, and students — new and previously unexpressed ideas began to be spoken at meetings and to appear in print, often without censorship or the "administrative measures" by the police that would have been automatic in Stalin's day. This "revolt of the mind," so termed by two Hungarians who shared in it,[3] was like a fresh wind blowing

World: Developments in the Post-Stalin Era (Notre Dame, Ind.: University of Notre Dame Press, 1962), were used with his permission as part of the Background Paper for the Seventh Midwest Seminar at Wingspread.

[3] Tamás Aczél and Tibor Meray, The Revolt of the Mind: A Case History

through the interstices of what had been a closed system. It led hitherto loyal Communists to question the official dogma as interpreted by their leaders and even to subject Marxism itself to revisionist criticism. It led writers to insist on a new freedom of inquiry and to seek personal and human values as against those that were politically imposed. It led to further resentment against Soviet domination of national life and therefore drew together some elements of the Communist elite with the mass of the population at least on this one issue of national self-expression. The rehabilitation of leaders condemned in the purge trials of the Stalin period, like Rajk in Hungary and Gomulka in Poland, provided occasion for national rejoicing. Unfortunately for Rajk, his rehabilitation was posthumous; he had been executed in 1949.

Significantly, the two nations where the thaw went furthest were Poland and Hungary. There the traditions of nationalism were very strong. In each case a homogeneous population, a deep anti-Soviet and anti-Russian feeling, and a strong Catholic tradition put the force of popular sentiment behind any tendency to assert national and individual rights against the suffocating totality of Soviet-Communist control. The confusion in party circles and the rivalry among Communist leaders led the regimes to temporize with challenges to their authority. Nor did they get any strong line from Moscow backing the repression of all such challenges; in fact, Khrushchev himself had become the symbol of anti-Stalinism through his "secret" speech of February 1956.

1956: The Year of Revolt

It was not apparent, when Khrushchev made that speech, what its results would be in Eastern Europe. Then in June anti-regime riots broke out in the city of Poznan in western Poland, only to be suppressed with the help of army units. The Poznan events had several significant aspects. First, the rioters were principally industrial workers, supposedly the mainstay of Communism. Second, their cry was not only for better wages and conditions; it was

of Intellectual Resistance behind the Iron Curtain (New York: Praeger, 1959).

also for liberty. Third, after digesting the meaning of the affair, the Polish government decided that it was more than the work of counterrevolutionary agents; that there were conditions that must be improved if the regime was to be able to live with its own people.

The climax in both Poland and Hungary came in October. Both revolutions posed a crisis for Communist rule and for the relationship with the Soviet Union. That they followed two distinct patterns, with different results, should not obscure the similarity of the issues at stake. For Khrushchev, his own rule in the Soviet Union not yet consolidated beyond all challenge, it was a question of how much to yield to satellite demands and when to take the ultimate resort to force. For the local Communist leaders, caught between Soviet and Communist imperatives and the pressures of their internal situation, the problem was how to keep their own footing among forces they could not easily control, if at all. For the Polish and Hungarian peoples, the choice was not always clear; what they wanted was plain enough — more freedom — but how they would react, what would be the mixture of restraint and wild hope, could not be predicted and depended largely on circumstance. Thus, following a thaw that had a similar pattern in both countries, the moment of crisis brought "Spring in October" to Poland and national tragedy to Hungary.

When Wladyslaw Gomulka came to power as the Polish Communist Party's first secretary, with a mandate for major change, a formidable delegation of high Soviet officials (including Khrushchev) descended upon Warsaw with demands that if accepted would have confirmed Poland's subordination in all respects to its eastern neighbor. The prospect was either a Polish capitulation or a Soviet resort to force to keep Poland from leaving the bloc, but the result was something different. Gomulka, knowing he had the backing of his party, of his army and police forces (by this time under reliable Polish control), and of the Polish people, courageously stood up to the Soviet leaders and insisted on the removal of both the symbols and the actuality of Soviet control of Poland's internal affairs. Khrushchev was not Stalin. He accepted

Gomulka's terms, provided that Poland would continue to harbor Soviet troops on Polish soil, to remain within the Soviet security system (of which the symbol was the Warsaw Pact of 1955), and to maintain the dominant position of the Communist Party. Both sides showed realism and restraint, as did the Polish people. As compared to what happened with Yugoslavia in 1948 or with Hungary in 1956, the compromise result may be attributed to the greater flexibility of Soviet policy, of which both sides were aware.

In Hungary, the crisis broke out in violence when a Stalinist-type Communist, Ernö Gerö, was still in power; he had a major responsibility for making violence inevitable. Imre Nagy, who might have played a role comparable to Gomulka's, came back into office when the situation was already out of hand, and he was never able to control it. From the start the Hungarian affair developed in a way which faced the Soviet leadership with the prospect that Hungary would throw off the Communist system altogether. There was no denying the depth of popular feeling against every sign of the Soviet presence, from the gigantic statue of Stalin which the crowd toppled over in Budapest to the ubiquitous red star that was cut out of every flag and replaced by the national symbol of Kossuth. The killings of Communist officials and security police and the fighting between Hungarians and Soviet troops must have convinced the Soviet leadership that compromise with the revolt would not be wise, indeed might not even be possible. When Imre Nagy agreed to the reconstitution of the non-Communist political parties, sought negotiations on the withdrawal of Soviet forces, and finally appealed to the United Nations to guarantee Hungary's neutrality, the decision was taken (or confirmed, if it had already been taken) to crush the revolt by overwhelming force in order to protect vital Soviet interests. It was a decision taken, also, in the near certainty that there would be no counter-intervention from the West.

The Hungarian revolt showed that a captive people could momentarily liberate themselves, but that they could not maintain their freedom in the face of Soviet military intervention. It showed also how badly the Communists had failed in trying to win the Hungarian people to their cause, for no Hungarians rallied to its defense save those who were totally committed to it and could expect no quarter from the people. Those who fought the Soviet soldiers in the streets of Budapest were mainly workers and students, the very ones who were supposedly the devotees of Communism. The desperate struggle of the Hungarian people, revealed to the world by the reports of the many Western correspondents and photographers who were there, tore apart the whole tissue of fabrication that made up the picture of Communist Eastern Europe which the Soviets had presented to the outside world. Yugoslav and Polish correspondents also reported the truth, which was published in the press of their own countries. After 1956 the Communist world was never quite the same again. Moscow kept Hungary within the bloc, but at heavy cost.

Elsewhere in Eastern Europe the Communist regimes appeared to survive the storm of 1956 with no more than a few anxious moments. There was student unrest in Rumania, especially in Transylvania where the large Hungarian minority was stirred by the struggle in neighboring Hungary. The Czech people saw the hopelessness of any attempt to revolt, and there was no Gomulka or Nagy among their Communist leaders. Bulgaria remained quiet under its iron-handed regime that was still basically Stalinist. Only in Poland and Hungary had conditions permitted the spectacular events that took place, and those two nations would be the bellwethers in the future. The dilution of Soviet centralized power in Eastern Europe and the erosion of Communist ideology had begun. The effects were bound to be felt throughout the whole Communist world.

Eastern Europe and the German Question

East Germany, the "German Democratic Republic," is a member of the Warsaw Pact and of the Soviet bloc's Council for Mutual Economic Assistance. In form of government it is a "people's democracy," that is, a dictatorship of the Socialist Unity (Communist) Party, whose leading strings are held in Moscow. Viewed from that standpoint, it is a satellite state like others in Eastern Europe, and a very important member of the Soviet bloc because of its geographic location, its industries, its resources, and its trained and educated people. Indeed, it is more of a puppet state than any of the others because its regime, headed by Walther Ulbricht, an old Comintern agent, is totally dependent on Moscow.

In other respects East Germany's situation is fundamentally different because it is not a "captive nation" in the same sense as Czechoslovakia or Bulgaria. It is a captive segment of a nation the greater part of which lives in freedom on the other side of the iron curtain and the Berlin wall. The partition of Germany, the result of the division of that country into separate zones of occupation at the close of the Second World War, hardened into semi-permanence when the cold war made its appearance and no peace treaty for Germany could be concluded. The German question remains on the agenda of the major allied powers of that war, whose representatives have discussed it at a series of conferences from Teheran in 1943 to Geneva in 1959. All the negotiations have failed for the basic reason that the Soviet Union has not been willing to give up its control over East Germany and is now wedded to the position that all concerned should recognize the fact of the existence of two Germanys, while the Western powers insist on the right of the German people to reunification in freedom. The former capital, Berlin, itself divided into Soviet and Western sectors though it is situated deep in East Germany, has become the neuralgic point of the whole unsolved problem, the point where Western positions are most vulnerable but must nevertheless be firmly held against Soviet threats and pressures because the fate of all Germany and Western Europe may depend on it.

The basic question has been who will control Germany. Free all-German elections would undoubtedly produce a pro-Western government that would associate itself with NATO, an outcome the Kremlin would not accept. Leaving the question to negotiations between the two German governments would give to the East German regime — that is to say, to the Soviet Union — a veto over all progress toward reunification and a means of exerting pressure on the Federal Republic. Khrushchev stated on a number of occasions that the only united Germany he could envisage was one which had disposed of the fascist and bourgeois elements in control of the Federal Republic, in other words, a Communist Germany. All the compromises put forward by one side or the other, or by third parties, have foundered on that basic difference. It is a difference that involves both principle (the Western conviction that the German people have the right to self-determination and that peace in Europe cannot be secure without it versus the Soviet conviction that Germany must eventually be won for the Communist world) and the strategic importance of German territory and German military potential in the world balance of power.

The unresolved German question has affected the fate of Eastern Europe in several ways. First, so long as the deadlock on Germany has persisted, the *status quo* in Eastern Europe — at least as far as Soviet-Western relations and negotiations are concerned — has tended to persist. The Soviets have been aware that once the two parts of Germany were reunited, the question of the status of Eastern Europe would be immediately posed. Second, the question of Germany is of special significance for two of the Eastern European states which have suffered from German aggression in the past and fear it in the future, Poland and Czechoslovakia. Third, the various proposals for disengagement in Central Europe have linked the status of the two parts of Germany with certain states of Eastern Europe, again Poland and Czechoslovakia primarily but also Hungary and others.

Poland, as the result of a Soviet decision ratified at the Potsdam conference in 1945, took over the administration of former German territories east of the line of the Oder and Western Neisse rivers (with the exception of Königsberg and the territory around it which the Soviet Union took for itself). The Potsdam agreement did not specifically sanction the Oder-Neisse line as legal boundary, merely stating that "the final delimitation of the western frontier of Poland should await the peace settlement." The Soviet Union and its satellites, including East Germany, have recognized it as the *de jure* frontier. The United States, Britain, and the German Federal Republic have continued to regard it as provisional.

This is no mere technical question for the Poles. Both regime and people are united in regarding the new "western territories" as permanently Polish and absolutely essential to Poland's national existence. Most of the original German inhabitants left at the end of the war, to be replaced by Poles from eastern territories lost to the Soviet Union and from other parts of Poland. Although the Federal Republic does not border on Poland and the boundary question does not arise now as a practical matter, it continues to be a source of worry to the Poles because of their fear that Germany, if and when reunited, will attempt to regain its lost territories. The activity of refugees from those territories who have carved out a place for themselves in the politics of the Bonn republic is anything but reassuring. The memories of German treatment of Poles during the recent war — and for centuries before it — naturally strengthen the feelings of fear and antagonism.

The Soviet Union has profited from this situation, which it knowingly helped to create, by assuming the role of protector of Poland against German *revanchisme*. Propaganda from Moscow and Warsaw has played the theme to a fare-thee-well, never letting the Polish people forget it and trying to distract them from the consequences of the Polish-Soviet relationship, which have included an amputation of Polish territory in the east, the imposition of a Communist regime, and the denial of an independent foreign policy.

Similar considerations apply, though to a lesser degree, to Czechoslovakia. There also centuries of antagonism, with the Czechs generally in the role of underdogs, have produced a fear and hatred of Germany which the Soviets and the Prague Communists have exploited. The Czechs experienced the tragedy of Munich and the later occupation by Nazi forces. At the end of the war the Czech government headed by President Beneš insisted on a mass expulsion of Germans from Czechoslovak territory and thus helped to create in the Federal Republic a large body of *Sudetendeutsch* refugees asserting rights to their old homeland. The whole problem — territorial, political, and psychological — has been less serious and less dangerous, however, than that between Germany and Poland. The Bonn government itself accepts the legality of the existing frontier and has made no territorial claims. But traditional Czech hostility to the Germans and friendliness to the Russians still serve Soviet purposes despite everything the Communists have done to alienate the population.

The situation of Hungary, Rumania, and Bulgaria, which were Germany's allies during the war, was quite different. They had no long and deeply rooted anti-German traditions. There were no German territorial claims against them. They did not feel any need for Russian protection against a resurgent Germany. With respect to those countries, therefore, the Western powers could proclaim themselves as supporters of self-determination both for the Germans, which meant reunification, and for the peoples of Eastern Europe, without adverse reaction from the latter. In Poland and Czechoslovakia, however, the peoples regarded self-determination for Germany as synonymous with the resurgence of German power and of mortal danger to themselves. That is the problem that the Western powers, including the Federal Republic, have faced in attempting to find an effective policy in Eastern Europe.

The numerous proposals for disengagement in Europe, which had a variety of motives, were directed partly to this problem of extracting the poison and the danger from the relations between the Germans and their eastern neighbors. Those which came from the eastern side, from the Soviet Union and Poland, were aimed primarily at preventing the growth of German military strength, whether of the Federal Republic or of a future united Germany. The authors of the Rapacki Plan, first proposed by Poland's foreign minister in 1957 at the United Nations and amended on later occasions, were well aware that West Germany was growing into the strongest power on the continent west of Russia and that the next step in its armament could be the acquisition of nuclear weapons. "Denuclearization" of a zone in Central Europe including West Germany, along with East Germany, Poland, and Czechoslovakia, was therefore the key provision of the Rapacki Plan.[4] Its most recent revision, the so-called Gomulka Plan, proposed as a first stage the freezing of nuclear armament levels in that area.[5] Major Soviet purposes were to weaken NATO and put a curb on West Germany, as well as to gain greater international recognition for East Germany and the *status quo* in Eastern Europe. The Polish government shared those purposes, and it may also have had an aim more strictly related to its own national interests: to gain more flexibility in foreign policy.

The Western powers, in rejecting the Rapacki Plan, stressed its military disadvantages for the entire NATO position in Europe. West Germany's territory and its armed forces are deemed essential to that position, and the application of the same limitations to East Germany, Poland, and Czechoslovakia would not be a sufficient counterweight. As a second factor, any arms limitation established on the basis of the present political units would seem to confirm the *status quo* and thus rule out the reunification of Germany. Those in the West who have backed the idea of disengagement, including leaders of the British Labour Party, have argued that it would relieve tensions, would represent a promising start toward wider disarmament, and might open the way for greater autonomy or independence for the Eastern European states. These supposed benefits have not been sufficiently attractive to the Western governments to induce them to embark on the experiment.

Disengagement may, however, offer the only way in which reunification of Germany can be brought about. Anthony Eden first linked the two questions in a suggestion made at the summit conference at Geneva in 1955, but it was not followed up. It has become customary to dismiss the possibility of reunification as unrealistic. Yet the hope for it touches a deep chord in all Germans. It is a problem that will not disappear with time. Since it is still a declared aim of the Western powers that Germany should be reunited in freedom, they may at some time come to the point of

[4] See Appendix F.
[5] See Appendix G.

considering what price, in the way of disengagement, they are willing to offer the Soviets in return. Some form of alliance-free status for a reunited Germany, backed by a security treaty that neither side could gain by breaking, might be a possibility. Part of such a settlement would be final acceptance on all sides of the Oder-Neisse line as the German-Polish frontier.

It should be stressed that the negotiation of any disengagement scheme would be extraordinarily difficult because of the large element of uncertainty in its practical results and the reluctance of both sides to gamble what they now have for something that might be much worse. The atmosphere of the cold war, which still prevails despite Soviet advocacy of peaceful coexistence and the few limited agreements that have been reached, would make it most difficult if not impossible to reach a general accord. The deadlock on Germany remains at the root of Soviet-Western relations. It might take a major change in Soviet policy toward Germany or in the situation in Eastern Europe to make disengagement politically possible.

II *UNITY AND DIVERSITY:*
RECENT POLITICAL TRENDS

The emphasis in this analysis of political trends will be on the forces of division, diversity, and nationalism that have so changed the face of Eastern Europe from the monolithic empire of Stalin's day. It is necessary therefore, in order to avoid any misunderstanding, to call attention to the continuing factors in the background that have set limits on how far those centrifugal forces could affect the basic situation which has prevailed since most of Eastern Europe came under Soviet and Communist control at the close of the Second World War.

Five nominally independent Eastern European states are still part of a bloc with the Soviet Union today: Poland, Czechoslovakia, Hungary, Rumania, and Bulgaria.[1] Whether they should also be considered as part of a larger bloc with Communist China, the Asian Communist states, and Albania is another question. From some standpoints, such as that of common hostility to the "capitalist world," they are all together, but the conflict between Moscow and Peking has created what are in fact two Communist blocs or "camps." The five Eastern European states remain in the Soviet military security system: two of them (Hungary and Po-

[1] East Germany is part of the bloc in that it also belongs to the Warsaw Pact and the Council for Mutual Economic Assistance and has a regime controlled by Moscow, but is left out of consideration in the analysis made in this chapter because of its special conditions. The Baltic states (Estonia, Latvia, Lithuania) are also not included because they are ruled directly as parts of the Soviet Union, though their independence is still recognized by the United States.

land), as well as East Germany, have Soviet troops stationed on their soil; all are members of the Warsaw Pact. All five are in close economic association with the Soviet Union in the Council for Mutual Economic Assistance (C.M.E.A. or Comecon). They follow the general Soviet line in international affairs, reject the Chinese brand of Communism, take their cue from Moscow and almost invariably vote with it at the United Nations and other international conferences.

Those five states are still under the control of their respective Communist parties, which have close relations with the Soviet Communist Party. Despite considerable relaxation, their governing regimes maintain the basic elements of totalitarian dictatorship built up in the Stalin period: one-party monopoly of political authority, control of the means of public communication, arbitrary exercise of police power, and the denial of human rights. The fact that they are unrepresentative minority regimes in their own countries makes for dependence on the Soviet Union, even though it is not a total dependence. Finally, the men in the Kremlin hold in their hands the ultimate sanction of overwhelming armed might by which they can enforce their will if they find it necessary, as was the case in Hungary in 1956.

Within the limits of that general background significant changes have taken place in Eastern Europe. The contrast with the situation a decade ago is striking. These changes have affected the methods, the instruments, and the effectiveness of Soviet control, the character and motivation of the Eastern European regimes, their relations with their own peoples, with each other, and with the West. It is not possible here to review in detail the developments of the last ten years, nor would it be useful to attempt to describe them country by country. The main events up to the year 1956 have already been mentioned. By taking a few general themes, with occasional concrete illustrations, we may highlight the main trends of the more recent period. Changes in Moscow were of capital importance, for in many ways it was Khrushchev's own policies that disrupted patterns in Eastern Europe.

The Effects of Soviet Policy and of Changes in the U.S.S.R.

From the very first days after Stalin's death his successors realized that they could not maintain all the rigidities of his system. In the period of their "collective" leadership, which was also a period of internal struggle for power, they introduced certain measures of decompression in the Soviet Union and let in a bit of fresh air. Similarly, as has already been pointed out, they found it impossible or unnecessary to maintain Stalin's system of direct domination over the Eastern European satellites through total penetration and control of their armed forces, government ministries, propaganda services, secret police, and of the ruling Communist parties. The elimination of Beria, chief of the Soviet security police, affected the security system in the satellite states as well as in the Soviet Union. Rivalry and jockeying among the other Soviet leaders, moreover, caused considerable confusion in the satellite Communist parties over where to look for direction. And as the search for new and less doctrinaire policies in the Soviet Union went forward, the Soviet leadership was willing to see some of the extreme policies of the "little Stalins" in Eastern Europe modified also. Hence Soviet consent to the "new course" in economic affairs adopted by most of the Eastern European states. Hence Soviet acquiescence in changes in their leadership. To take the most striking example, in 1953 the Soviet leaders themselves designated Imre Nagy, who was to become a symbol of nationalism and of reform, to succeed the Stalinist Mátyás Rákosi as premier of Hungary.

The whole process of "de-Stalinization" touched off by Khrushchev's speech in February 1956 contributed to the tremendous uncertainty and confusion already apparent in the Eastern European states and especially in their Communist parties. Those leaders who had been Stalin's chief lieutenants found their position undermined. At the same time, they were the ones who over the years had been the most subservient and often the most useful to Moscow. They, with Stalin's support, had carried out drastic purges within their parties. Now the discrediting of Stalin brought to gale force the pressures for rehabilitation of the victims of the purges and for punishment of those responsible. Factionalism within the parties, with Khrushchevists arrayed against Stalinists and nationalists against Muscovites, tended to break down internal discipline, open doors to non-Communist influences in national affairs, and weaken Moscow's authority. The culmination of these trends came with the crisis of 1956 in Poland and in Hungary.

While the Soviet bloc survived that crisis, it has never been the same since. The outcome of Khrushchev's confrontation with the new Communist leadership in Poland, as we have seen, was a new kind of compromise by which Moscow in effect recognized Poland's internal autonomy in return for Poland's continued acceptance of the essentials of the Soviet position in international affairs. That bargain is still being kept on both sides. The Soviets have also moved toward the same kind of compromise in Hungary, even though János Kádár, who has the leading position in that country, is the very man who was installed as a Soviet puppet at the time the popular revolt of 1956 was crushed. By relying on the ability of leaders like Gomulka and Kádár to run their own countries and keep them in line on the basic issues, however, and thus introducing a greater element of consent into the Soviet-satellite relationship, the Soviets created obvious difficulties for other Communist parties whose outlook and organization were still basically Stalinist. These difficulties Khrushchev compounded by his renewed attack on Stalin at the Twenty-second Congress of the Soviet Communist Party in the autumn of 1961. It led to new purges in the Bulgarian party, as well as in Hungary. It created embarrassment for leaders such as Antonín Novotný in Czechoslovakia, who was noted for his subservience to Moscow and now found himself pushed by Khrushchev's own policies to open up the record of the past and contemplate the sacrifice not only of the inanimate symbols of Stalinism, such as the huge Stalin monument in Prague, but also of its living remnants.

The uncertainty and factionalism which have appeared in the Communist parties of Eastern Europe are thus in many ways the result of the inconsistencies, shifts, and changes that have taken place in the Soviet Union and in Soviet policy. Because of the gulf that separated them from their own peoples, those parties were particularly vulnerable to such changes taking place at the center of the world Communist movement. They were also, and inevitably, affected by what was happening in their own countries, by the practical problems of governing and staying in power. Here they had to consider whether and how far they could come to terms with a force which up to the period of Communist rule had been recognized as a primary motive element in those societies, whether it took the form of deeply held popular feelings and desires or of organized political movements and governmental policies. That force was nationalism.

The Resurgence of Nationalism

The nationalist leaders and parties seeking to play a role in the countries of Eastern Europe after the Second World War were pushed aside and destroyed by the Communists, who had all kinds of support from the Soviet Union including the menacing presence of Soviet armed forces. During the early period of Communist rule nationalism was condemned as a bourgeois phenomenon and suppressed as an organized political force. The Communists proclaimed that under the new socialist order all nationalities would freely and fraternally cooperate with each other and with the Soviet Union.

Consciousness of nationality, however, cannot so easily be dealt with by fiat. Popular opposition to Soviet domination, rooted in the longing for national independence and self-expression, remained. After Stalin's death, with the easing of the terror and the limited loosening of censorship and thought-control, many in the party and "front" organizations themselves began to question the slavish adoption of Soviet models in everything from economic planning to lyric poetry and to accommodate themselves at least in some slight degree to the opinions of the people. Especially among the intellectuals, including those within the Communist parties, there were instances of an amazingly outspoken opposition to the prevailing ideological conformity.

The influence of Tito's Yugoslavia on the rest of Eastern Europe cannot be precisely measured but it was undoubtedly a disruptive element within the Communist movements, affecting both the leadership and the rank and file. Tito proved after 1948 that a Communist country could declare its independence of Moscow and make the decision stick. He practiced national Communism, even though he avoided the term. And despite Stalin's purges of prominent Communists who were or might be attracted by Tito's example, elements of national Communism were still present in the other Eastern European Communist parties. Indeed, the mere fact that their leaders were trying to exercise effective political power in their countries, at a time when they were beset by many problems and could get only uncertain guidance from outside, led them to undertake new policies and to make concessions that took account of some of the realities of their national environment. Thus elements of nationalism worked their way into the Communist parties and regimes.

The events of 1956 were a confirmation of that fact. Following Khrushchev's reconciliation with Tito in 1955 and 1956 in which he accepted Yugoslavia's independence and Tito's thesis of separate roads to socialism, it was virtually impossible to calm the increasing popular unrest developing in Poland and Hungary or to contain the pressures for a more vigorous assertion of national interests. When Gomulka took over the leadership of the Polish Workers' (Communist) Party in October, he did so as a Polish Communist determined to assert independence from Soviet dictation in Poland's affairs. In that aim he had the support of the Polish people, who would also have liked to assert Poland's freedom from Communism but could not. In Hungary, where a movement of protest grew into open revolt, Imre Nagy was cast in the role of a national Communist, but he was caught between the tide of popular opposition to the whole Communist system and the Soviet determination to use force to keep Hungary from repudiating Communism altogether and leaving the bloc.

In attempting to reconstruct the bloc after the scare of 1956 that threatened its dissolution, Khrushchev used the term "socialist commonwealth," which in itself was a concession to the idea of separate national roads to socialism. Unity under Soviet leadership was deemed essential, but the diversity permitted was broad enough to include a Poland which was a standing invitation to other Eastern European states to demand greater domestic autonomy. It was broad enough to include a Hungary where the regime chose to make a kind of tacit armistice with the people, taking into account their longing for surcease from Communist exhortation and pressure and for more tolerable conditions of material and intellectual life. It is significant that Kádár, trying to live down or explain away his role of renegade and traitor in the climactic days of November 1956, plays up his role before 1956, when he was in jail at the hands of the hated Stalinist leader of that time, Rákosi. If he cannot rightly be called a national Communist, he gives certain signs of acting like one in response to popular pressures and nationalist feelings in Hungary which have demonstrated how dangerous they can be when totally repressed.

The force of nationalism exists in the other Eastern European states as well. In each it expresses itself at different times and sometimes in different ways, for each has its own history, traditions, and national character. In Czechoslovakia, which seemed for so long to be quietly submissive under the rule of the same leaders who had maintained themselves in power since Stalin's day, economic troubles and outspoken criticism within and without the Communist Party have caused the regime to condemn parts of its past record and to sacrifice some of its most prominent figures. In Rumania, which despite some purges has had a continuity of top leadership going all the way back to the Communist seizure of power, that leadership itself has played for popular support and made itself a champion of national interests against interference by other states of the Soviet bloc.

The Rumanian case, which has centered on the issue of economic independence, the right of a Communist regime to make its own decisions on the development of its national economy without dictation or interference by the Soviet Union or by any bloc-wide supranational authority, will be discussed in the following chapter on economic factors. Here it should be noted that political factors frequently lie behind economic decisions and that important political consequences flow from them. In Rumania, the insistence of Gheorghiu-Dej and his colleagues on carrying out their economic program and their cultivation of trade with the West were in consonance with cautious but still noticeable trends in the political and cultural fields: changes within the Communist Party, a separate line on the Sino-Soviet controversy, signs of independence in voting at the United Nations, rewriting of the official version of recent history, reduction of Soviet cultural influence, and closer ties with Yugoslavia. These may not be major changes, but they seem indicative of a trend.

Nationalism has many faces and many aspects. As an unquenchable fire in the spirits of the peoples of Eastern Europe, it is a factor of continuing opposition to domination from outside. This is the lesson of a long history during which these small nations have struggled for their national existence against the great empires of Austria, Turkey, Russia, and Germany, against the domination of Hitler, and then against that of the Soviet Union.

Nationalism has thus been an element of strength for Eastern Europe. But it has also been an element of weakness, as national rivalries, antagonisms, claims and counterclaims have throughout modern history turned the nations of the region against each other. The most bitter conflicts have been those between neighbors over territory, boundaries, and the treatment of national minorities. These conflicts, which take place within as well as between the states of Eastern Europe, have in the past exhausted the energies of nations, destroyed the possibility of cooperative regional solutions to their problems, and made them a prey for outside powers seeking strategic advantage.

The Communist conquest of the whole area temporarily pushed those struggles below the surface of politics. The Soviets encouraged nationalism in Eastern Europe only when it could be used against some state outside the bloc. Thus they tried to use against Greece the grievances of its Slavic Macedonian minority and the irredentism of its Balkan neighbors. They helped, as we have seen, to keep Polish and Czech bitterness against Germany at a high pitch, directing it against West Germany only. After 1948, when Tito had become an enemy instead of an ally, they opened the door to Bulgarian and Albanian agitation and the revival of their time-worn claims to Yugoslav territory. Among states of the bloc, however, the lid was kept on.

Now, as the Eastern European regimes take on greater national coloration and seek popularity at home, more is heard of the old nationality disputes. The Soviet Union has not had the will or the authority to prevent it. As an example, the Hungarian minority in Rumania, for years treated with kid gloves, has seen its touted "autonomous region" cut down both in area and in autonomy. The separate Hungarian university at Cluj in Transylvania has lost its special status by being absorbed into the Rumanian university. Ever since 1956, when Rumania felt the shock of events across the frontier in Hungary, its regime has been more aggressively nationalistic, and this issue has clouded relations between the countries.

Czechoslovakia also has a Hungarian minority, long a source of potential trouble, of which it unsuccessfully tried to rid itself by expulsions and an exchange of population in the aftermath of the Second World War. Even more significant has been the long-standing conflict between Czechoslovak centralism and Slovak nationalism, which existed in the prewar republic and exists within the Communist state and party structure of today. The national issue injects itself into other controversial questions and intensifies factionalism.

The prime example of the effect of local nationalism on Communist solidarity is Albania. Across the frontier in Yugoslavia lies a territory peopled largely by Albanians, and Yugoslavia, for many years and under various regimes, has been regarded by Albanians as a threat to their country's existence. Consequently, hostility toward its larger neighbor has been a prime motive force in Albanian policy. After the Tito-Stalin break in 1948 Albania's leader, Enver Hoxha, became Stalin's loudest and most violent supporter against the Yugoslav heresy. When Khrushchev tried to make up with Tito in the mid-fifties, Hoxha was the most reluctant of the satellites' leaders to go along. In the past few years, as Khrushchev fell out with Communist China and turned toward closer relations with Yugoslavia, Albania made its choice for China and invited virtual expulsion from the Soviet part of the bloc. Throughout its short history as a national state Albania, regardless of ideological factors, has always sought support from a big power far enough away not to be a threat itself but able to check or eliminate the threats of those close at hand.

All these signs of the revival or persistence of local nationalism in Eastern Europe may or may not prove an ultimate benefit to its peoples. But they surely represent a weakening and tearing of the fabric of Communist solidarity. They illustrate the difficulties posed to Moscow and to the Communist regimes themselves. The latter are drawn to using the force of nationalism, though basically they are afraid of it, and rightly so.

Effects of the Soviet-Chinese Rift

The facts of geography and of power and the idea of national interest have held the Eastern European states on the Soviet side in the Moscow-Peking dispute. On the ideological issues, the Soviet line on peaceful coexistence, the need to avoid nuclear war, and the ability of socialism to win by peaceful competition suits their leaders far more than does the Chinese emphasis on violent revolution, a worldwide Communist offensive, and accepting the risks of war. As small states, furthermore, they are not so concerned as either Moscow or Peking about the world struggle against capitalism; hopeful for a period of stability in which to develop, they are not anxious to heat up crisis situations in Berlin (here East Germany is the exception) or elsewhere.

Yet though they may stand with the Soviet Union against China, there is no doubt that the existence of the conflict between the two big powers of the Communist world has given the smaller ones additional room for maneuver. Poland attempted to take advantage of Soviet-Chinese differences in 1956–57, even before they had really crystallized. Albania, as we have seen, went the whole way and took a jump into the Chinese camp which the Kremlin was unable to prevent or reverse. Rumania has provided another kind of illustration: how an Eastern European state can take advantage of the dispute to advance its own interests without altering its basic orientation. The Rumanian regime, while engaged in a controversy with the Soviet Union on economic matters, did not hesitate to conclude trade and cultural agreements with Communist China and to send an ambassador to Albania, where no other state of the Soviet camp had had similar representation since they followed Moscow's virtual break in relations with Tirana in 1961 by recalling their own ambassadors. These steps, taken independently, were a sign of increased freedom of action and of greater bargaining power.

The Soviet-Chinese dispute, furthermore, has brought into question the unity of ideology which supposedly lay at the heart of the solidarity of the bloc. There is now no longer any recognized center which sets the line for the world Communist movement. So long as "polycentrism" was just theory by Italy's Communist leader Togliatti or practice by Tito, it did not shake Moscow's authority seriously, but the emergence of Peking as a rival source of the party line greatly diminished the Soviet Communist Party's ideological primacy even among those parties in the bloc which took its side against the Chinese. The Soviet party found in 1964 that it was unable to rally them in a common front to condemn China's "dogmatism."

The split thus contributed to questioning and factionalism in the Communist parties of Eastern Europe. Although the Chinese experiment with communes and the "great leap forward" attracted interest and a following in some states (notably Bulgaria), there is no evidence of the formation of pro-Chinese factions in any Eastern European party except the Albanian. What the Chinese challenge to Moscow has done is to weaken the latter's authority and to diminish the significance of ideology as glue to hold the Communist states on the same line. The European parties continue to regard themselves as Communist and to conform to most Soviet policies, but the decline in ideology has resulted in a greater flexibility in matters of practical action.

The Continuing Independence of Yugoslavia

Soviet-Yugoslav relations have undergone a succession of ups and downs, of alternating conflict and reconciliation, which may not have reached its end. At the present juncture there has been a rapprochement between them which appears to be based on common hostility to Chinese positions, Khrushchev's acceptance of Yugoslavia as a socialist state, and Tito's conviction that Soviet policies both internal and foreign are evolving in directions compatible with Yugoslav interests. Yugoslavia now supports Soviet positions on most, but not all, international questions. But it does so because the Tito regime believes it to be in the Yugoslav interest. Yugoslavia has not given up its independence of decision in foreign policy any more than in domestic policy, where the differences with the Soviet Union are striking.

The fact that Yugoslavia has moved into close association with the bloc while not really rejoining it (it remains outside the Warsaw Pact and plays only a limited role in the C.M.E.A.) could have portentous consequences for the solidarity of the bloc and Moscow's directing role. Yugoslavia now has relations with the other Eastern European states on both the diplomatic and the party level. Its representatives are invited to Communist Party congresses. Their privileged independent position will be constantly before the eyes of Communists from Poland, Czechoslovakia, and the others. If the Soviets welcome Tito back into the fold, it may seem to jeopardize Yugoslavia's hard-earned independence. But if this is done on Tito's terms, which ensure that independence, one may ask what kind of fold the Soviet bloc has become.

The basis of Yugoslav foreign policy is nonalignment. In some ways this neutralism may serve Soviet purposes, if for example it helps the Soviet anti-Western and anti-Chinese campaign in Asia and Africa. But it is surely also a danger. A Communist state flaunting its opposition to blocs, totally out of Soviet control in its doctrines and its policies, and taking aid from the West is hardly a comfortable colleague in the "international workers' movement" in which guidance is supposed to come from Moscow.

Yugoslavia is developing ties with Rumania, especially in the economic sphere where they have agreed on a huge joint project, wholly outside the C.M.E.A. framework, for the development of transport and power on the Danube River. The Yugoslavs are also receptive to talk of an atom-free security zone in the Balkans such as was proposed originally by Rumania several years ago. Such developments may in some respects be useful to Moscow; in other respects they may not. The prospective association of Yugoslavia with other Balkan and Eastern European states in a federation or customs union in 1947 and 1948 was one of Stalin's main reasons for turning on Tito. Nor was Khrushchev any more willing to see Yugoslavia organize some kind of Balkan bloc that could be independent of his decisions.

The fact of Yugoslav independence, regardless of the impact of particular policies, is bound to influence the other Eastern European countries in the future as it has in the past. The closer the contacts between them, the stronger that influence is likely to be.

Conclusions

It is obvious that in the past few years many crosscurrents have affected the countries of Eastern Europe and their ruling Communist parties. The shifts and zigzags in Soviet policy, the dispute between the Soviet Union and Communist China, the influence of Yugoslavia, the combination of rapid industrial growth and major unsolved economic problems, the interaction of economics and politics — to which should be added personal rivalries among leaders and the whole tangled web of plot and counterplot that is a legacy of the past — all these influences have shaken the structure of Communist Eastern Europe. They have weakened Soviet authority. They have increased conflicts among the states and factionalism within each of them. Ideological discipline has seriously declined. Each Communist party has what might be called its Stalinists, its moderates, and its revisionists, with other factions in between.

It is true that Nikita Khrushchev was at the helm in Moscow while many of these changes took place. He was the first to explode the myths and the authority of Stalinism. He himself became the symbol of the new order. But in actuality he did not shape it; indeed, there was scarcely any order at all. Khrushchev presided over the twists and turns of doctrine and of policy, but in the evolution of Eastern Europe he was more the creature than the creator of events. His successors are hardly more likely than he to find the key to mastery of a situation that has changed irretrievably since Stalin's time.

It is risky to speak generally of trends in Eastern Europe. While there are important common factors which push the different states one way or restrain them in another, the main impression is one of diversity. Within certain obvious limitations common to all, each country is moving along paths peculiar to itself, conditioned by its own history, the character of its people, and the special circumstances of its relations with the Soviet Union, with its neighbors, and with the West. Whether the trend is called national Communism or something else does not greatly matter. Certainly the idea of national interest has grown stronger in these Communist regimes, even though they came to their positions of authority as bearers of an alien ideology and with the help of an outside power, on which their existence still largely depends.

The foregoing conclusions, if they are valid, raise the question whether the Eastern European states can still properly be called satellites. What their spokesmen say in public statements and in the press gives little reason for calling them anything else. In their military alignment and in the general lines of foreign policy they are still in Moscow's orbit. Nevertheless, the Kremlin's control is by no means absolute. It must exert its influence in much the same ways as any great power does in dealing with much smaller and weaker neighboring states: by utilizing the facts of geography and the disparity in power and resources, by economic pressures or economic aid, by appeals to common interest, and by the existence of overwhelming military strength in the background. It cannot do it by unquestioned and unquestionable orders delivered from the central authority of an international ideological movement and carried out by a reliable and efficient political apparatus.

It is not apparent, however, despite the greater independence shown by their governments, that the Eastern European states can reach either of two critical points, both of which are of enormous importance with respect to the consequences the process of change may have in reducing the Communist threat to the West and serving the cause of peace. The first is the point at which a state acquires control of its own foreign policy, as Yugoslavia did. Poland, Rumania, and others have shown signs of independence on various occasions, especially on matters of foreign trade. But on their basic alignment, none has had freedom of choice. None has been able to choose neutrality between East and West, as Hungary tried and failed to do in 1956. The second point as yet not reached is that at which the monopoly of political power held by a Communist party is broken. That is not a necessary criterion of independence, as the case of Yugoslavia has shown. Yet it is not entirely an internal matter so long as the Communist ideology and the "international workers' movement" affect the foreign policies of states. And it is a criterion of true political freedom for the peoples of Eastern Europe.

The possibility that one of those points on the way to national independence and a freer society may be reached and passed, perhaps imperceptibly as one in a long and gradual series of steps, need not be ruled out, implausible as it may seem now. Some of the most striking events in the history of the Communist world — Tito's break with Stalin in 1948, the outbreak and early success of the Hungarian popular revolt of 1956, and the defection of Albania in 1960 — were not foreseen in the West and were scarcely believed when they happened. In any event, that centrifugal forces are at work in the Soviet bloc today is beyond question. The trend toward autonomy and self-assertion on the part of the Eastern European states is a fact of international life, not easily reversed. How it will develop in the future depends in large measure on events outside the area itself: on trends within the Soviet Union, on the directions taken by Soviet policy, and on the policies of the West.

III *ECONOMIC FACTORS*

PRIOR to the Second World War the countries of Eastern Europe, while varying considerably among themselves, generally had less well developed economies and lower standards of living than those of Western Europe. Only the western parts of Czechoslovakia, and to a lesser extent Poland and Hungary, had shown any substantial industrial growth. All were basically peasant countries with a heavy proportion of the population engaged in an agriculture that was not very efficient either where the system was one of large estates or where small peasant holdings prevailed.

Eastern Europe's trade was largely with Western Europe, to which it supplied food and raw materials in return for manufactured goods. During the depression years of the 1930s Germany gained a leading position in the area because it alone could provide a market for Eastern Europe's exports. Then during the war the resources of these countries were harnessed to Germany's military needs, whether they were defeated states occupied by the Germans (Poland, Czechoslovakia, Yugoslavia, Albania) or were Germany's allies and satellites (Hungary, Rumania, Bulgaria).

The Turn Eastward

During the closing months of the war Soviet rule supplanted German rule in most of Eastern Europe. The first concern of the Soviet Union, beyond assuring itself a preponderant political position, was to exploit the available resources for the rebuilding of its own economy. This was done under the guise of occupation costs, reparation for war damage, restitution of stolen property, and the seizure as "German assets" of all kinds of goods and installations that had been in German hands during the war. This process of taking bore more heavily on the former German satellites than on the others, but two of the latter, Poland and Yugoslavia, had undergone great war damage themselves and were dependent on help from the West, through the United Nations Relief and Rehabilitation Administration, to get economic life started again.

A favorite Soviet device during this early period was the bilateral joint company, by which a whole sector of a country's economy (e.g., transport, oil, banking) would be placed under the control of a "50-50" company which was in fact run by the Soviets. Contribution to capital by the smaller partner came from its own assets, while the Soviet Union contributed "German assets" which it claimed as its own. The joint companies were most widely used in Rumania but they appeared on the scene in Hungary and Bulgaria too, and even in Yugoslavia. Resources like uranium production were simply taken over directly by the Soviet Union.

The terms of trade were another though less flagrant means of exploitation. The trade of Eastern Europe,[1] because of the new political situation, was shifted sharply eastward. Where before the war (1938) it had been 64 per cent with the West, chiefly with Western Europe, and less than 2 per cent with the U.S.S.R., by 1948 it was already roughly 30 per cent with the U.S.S.R. and over 50 per cent within the bloc. By 1955 the direction of trade of the five satellites was as shown at the top of the next page.[2]

This trade was all arranged by bilateral negotiations between the Soviet government and each satellite regime. The latter countries had little or no bargaining power even should they have

[1] Eastern Europe here includes Albania, Bulgaria, Czechoslovakia, Hungary, Poland, Rumania, and Yugoslavia. For later years (after 1948) Yugoslavia is not included. East Germany is left out because its trade with West Germany makes it a special case, although the overall trend is the same as for the others.

[2] The tabulation is based on *Direction of International Trade, Statistical Papers*, Series T, Vol. IX, No. 10 (New York: United Nations, 1958), pp. 161–78.

Percentage of Total Trade

	With the U.S.S.R.	Within the Bloc (including U.S.S.R. and China)
Poland	32	43
Czechoslovakia	35	70
Hungary	30	61
Rumania	54	82
Bulgaria	49	89

wanted to exercise any. The prices and other terms were in fact dictated by the Soviet government to its own advantage. As one flagrant example, Poland sold coal to the Soviet Union at a fixed price less than one-tenth of the world price; at the same time the iron ore which Poland had to get from the Soviet Union was purchased at the world price or higher.

During the Stalinist period, moreover, the satellite regimes adopted plans and policies for their domestic economies which combined an imposed social revolution with a slavish copying of the Soviet model of the march to socialism. Each regime set out on the path of central planning, rapid industrialization, and agricultural collectivization regardless of the economic consequences. All of this meant that these new "people's democracies," supposedly states of the workers and peasants, were in fact ruthlessly exploiting workers and peasants as well as the "feudal remnants" and the old bourgeoisie. By the time of Stalin's death the economies were so strained and the people so embittered that changes had to be made. Hence the "new course" adopted first in East Germany and Hungary and then in most of the other states, leading to some slackening of the rush to build heavy industries and to force the peasants into collectives. But the main result of these changes, as of the intellectual "thaw" and of the slackening of police terror, was great uncertainty on the part of both leadership and people, an uncertainty that contributed to the dramatic events of 1956 in Poland and Hungary.

Yugoslavia's Separate Road

Yugoslavia, meanwhile, was providing an example of the benefits of national independence. When they were thrown out of the

Communist bloc in 1948 because they would not give up their independence, the Yugoslav leaders had publicly denounced the Soviet Union for its attempts to exploit their country economically through the device of joint companies and in other ways. Yugoslavia had then been made the object of economic warfare by the Kremlin and the satellite regimes, but it turned to the West for economic aid and received it.

Of particular significance for the other regimes of Eastern Europe was the fact that Yugoslavia had not had to sell its independence in return for Western help. On the contrary, it maintained its character as a socialist state, albeit one which was diverging more and more from the Soviet model. In their struggle with Stalin and the Cominform the Yugoslav leaders found that they had to take more account than they ever had before of the temper of their own people and of local conditions. Consequently, they began to develop new institutions, notably the workers' councils, and to pay more attention to more economical use of their strained resources. Under pressure from the peasants they found it expedient to give up the idea of rapid socialization of the countryside and allowed the peasants to withdraw from collective farms. Practically all of them did. Tito's separate road was also marked by decentralization of economic planning, greater powers of decision for individual enterprises, some use of the free market, more balanced development, and a greater concern for the consumer.

Yugoslavia's turn from East to West, of course, was a matter of necessity. So long as no trade or other economic relations with the East were possible, Tito had to make the shift or else go under. But the more significant fact was that Yugoslavia was able to meet its real economic needs so much better in association with the free-world economic system than as part of the closed system of the Communist bloc. It was not just a matter of getting Western grants and loans. Yugoslavia found better outlets for its exports. It joined in the operations of international economic organizations and agencies, both those under the United Nations umbrella and those of the Western European region (such as the Organization for European Economic Cooperation and the European Payments Union). It developed useful economic ties with many of the developing countries. All in all, it established an economic position for itself that enabled it to renew normal relations with the Soviet Union and the bloc, when the time came for that, on Yugoslavia's own terms which included keeping the ties with the West. In recent years, regardless of political shifts, Yugoslavia has had a rather stable trade pattern, over 50 per cent of its trade being with the West and from 25 to 30 per cent with the Soviet bloc.

The New Economic Situation of Eastern Europe after 1956

In reappraising its relations with the satellites after the crisis of 1956 the Soviet Union saw the need for important changes in economic policies, particularly toward the two states that had caused all the trouble, Poland and Hungary. One result of the review by Khrushchev and Gomulka of the whole gamut of Polish-Soviet relations was a revision of the earlier arrangements under which the Soviet Union, as Poland's chief trading partner, bought at fixed low prices and sold at high ones. The Soviet Union paid a lump sum of $525 million in a cancellation of debts against counterclaims, which was in fact compensation for past discrimination; it negotiated a new trade agreement, and extended credits to Poland totaling $320 million (mainly in rubles). It was clearly Khrushchev's view that the period of exploitation was over and that if future trouble was to be avoided the "socialist commonwealth" would have to have an economic basis more acceptable to its Eastern European members than the old Stalinist system.

With Hungary, its economy disrupted by the follies of the Rákosi period and by the revolution, Khrushchev also had to find new and more suitable economic policies. The new Kádár regime, trying to establish itself in the face of the sullen noncooperation of the populace, especially the industrial workers who continued to resist long after the fighting was over, needed emergency help. The Soviet Union, as in the case of Poland, came through with food shipments, new trade arrangements favorable to Hungary, and loans. Total credits for the period 1956–57 were in the neighborhood of $288 million.

Behind these shifts in economic policy was a political compulsion: to stabilize Soviet-satellite relations on a basis that would ensure the cooperation of the satellite governments and at the same time consolidate the position of those governments with their own populations. There was no assurance of success, however, for the strengthening of their position did not guarantee their continuing allegiance to the Soviet Union; it would increase their bargaining power, which in due course they might use against the Soviet Union if they chose. It was quite natural that the Soviets also turned toward the idea of greater economic integration of the bloc, which would tie the satellite economies so closely to the Soviet economy that they could not afford to show much independence.

On the Western side, the events of 1956 in Poland evoked a new departure in American policy. At the time of the Polish October, President Dwight Eisenhower and Secretary of State John Foster Dulles had said that the United States would be willing to provide economic sustenance for the independence of Eastern European states. Poland did not win full independence, but its stand was deemed sufficient to justify American aid. The United States did not move very quickly but it was receptive to Poland's request, and after some months of negotiation, in June and August of 1957 it concluded agreements to sell $65 million worth of surplus agricultural products to Poland for local currency and to extend an Export-Import loan of $30 million for other food products, mining machinery, and transportation. Roughly the same arrangement was continued in the following years. By the end of 1961 the United States had made available to Poland $410 million in agricultural commodities and $61 million in long-term credits.[3]

For the United States, economic aid to Poland was an exception to policy toward the rest of the bloc, and it was an experi-

[3] *Department of State Bulletin*, Vol. XLVI, No. 1175, January 1, 1962, p. 35.

ment. Its justification was twofold: that it would strengthen the Gomulka regime in its semi-independent position and that it would show the deep American interest in the welfare of the Polish people. Gomulka has not been perceptibly friendly to the West and after an initial period of mild self-assertion has closely followed the line of Soviet foreign policy. But the Polish economy has followed its own path, which has included private peasant farming as the basis of the agricultural system, a unique phenomenon in the Soviet bloc.

For political reasons the United States was not prepared to aid Hungary after 1956, nor any other state of the bloc. Yet the assistance extended to Poland, like that to Yugoslavia, stood as evidence to all those states that there were economic lines to the West open to them if they made progress along the path toward independence. Whether Moscow opposed or condoned Poland's acceptance of American aid is not clear. Khrushchev's denunciation of Yugoslavia's attempt to build socialism with capitalist dollars suggests the answer. In any case it remained a delicate operation for all concerned, not least the executive branch of the American government, which faced growing opposition in the Congress to its policy of aid to Poland and to Yugoslavia as well.

C.M.E.A. and the Economic Integration of the Bloc

After 1956, with the new "socialist commonwealth" resting less on domination and more on consent than before, the Soviet leaders saw the need of knitting it together with bonds of economic interest while at the same time increasing the overall economic effort. They also wished to prevent any damaging effects which increasing economic ties with the West might have on the solidarity of the bloc. Accordingly, they seized on the existing but more or less dormant Council for Mutual Economic Assistance as the best available multilateral instrument for achieving their purposes. Up to then it had been used mainly for coordinating trade arrangements and exchanging information.

In 1957, for the first time, the members of the C.M.E.A. (the

Soviet Union and all the European satellites, but not Communist China) agreed in general terms to coordinate national economic plans and targets, create a multilateral clearing system, increase mutual technical aid, and develop specialization in production according to a rational division of labor among the member states. It was easier to announce these objectives than to reach them. They were restated at meetings in 1958 and 1959, then were enshrined in the formal C.M.E.A. statute adopted in 1960. Commissions were established to deal with a host of separate industries and products, and they have since set a feverish pace of activity.

Table 1. Trade of Eastern Europe,* 1957–61
(in millions of dollars)

Year	Trade with Free World		Trade within Communist Bloc	
	Exports	Imports	Exports	Imports
1957	1,520	1,567	3,683	4,025
1958	1,691	1,634	4,115	3,999
1959	1,774	1,853	4,784	4,893
1960	2,146	2,174	5,271	5,429
1961	2,373	2,384	5,753	6,924

SOURCES: *Mutual Defense Assistance Control Act of 1951, Reports of the Administrator to Congress* (Washington, D.C.: Government Printing Office), 15th Report, 1962, Table 2, p. 36 and 16th Report, 1963, Table 4, p. 65; *Yearbook of International Trade Statistics 1962* (New York: United Nations, 1964), Table A, pp. 14–15; *Direction of International Trade, Statistical Papers*, Series T, Vol. XI, No. 9 (New York: United Nations, 1960), p. 235. Because of the variety of statistical sources from which these totals are computed, they must be considered as approximate rather than precise.
*Includes Albania and East Germany.

Intra-bloc trade increased between 1957 and 1961, but so did Eastern Europe's trade with the outside world, as Table 1 shows. The progress toward a C.M.E.A. multilateral trade and payment system was slight. Information on national economic plans was exchanged by the participants, but only after they had been adopted. There were bilateral or tripartite agreements on production of some items (especially among Poland, Czechoslovakia, and East Germany). The "Friendship Oil Pipeline," to bring Soviet oil to Central and East Europe, was begun, and a power grid linking the western districts of the U.S.S.R. with some of the satellites was established. But this was relatively minor progress toward integration. By 1962 the time was ripe for some more positive steps in that direction; this was the view of some of the satellite governments, including East Germany, Czechoslovakia, and Poland, as well as of the Soviet leadership.

At this time Western Europe was already making great economic strides ahead, largely because of the strength shown by the Common Market and its member states. The Common Market by its very existence presented a challenge to the Communists. They could and did denounce it in their propaganda as the last gasp of monopoly capitalism confronting the inevitable victory of socialism. But they had to do something about the economic realities with which they were confronted. For the Eastern European regimes, the Common Market, as a regional bloc discriminating against outsiders, might disrupt what trade they had with the West, which was necessary to their industrial development. A united Western Europe might prove too powerful to bargain with. For the Soviet Union, the Common Market might become a formidable enemy and an attractive force both on the states of Eastern Europe and on the nonaligned. Further integration of the bloc was one answer.

A meeting of governmental and party chiefs of the C.M.E.A. countries in June 1962 laid down the principles of the international socialist division of labor which were to guide the development of the bloc. The basic idea made good economic sense: each country was to produce that for which it was best fitted and all would benefit accordingly. The real questions concerned the making of decisions, especially on investment, for here were a number of separate national economies at different stages of economic growth, each one with its annual and long-term plans. The institutional proposals adopted in 1962 provided for an Executive Committee of permanent high-level representatives to make the necessary decisions on the detailed and integrated planning for the bloc as a whole, an incredibly difficult job in view of the varying price systems, investment plans, trade patterns, and, above all, political factors, which were leading in the direction of national autonomy rather than integration. Each national regime was understandably reluctant to give up the power of decision on matters vitally affecting the development of its own economy. Thus, the less developed nations feared being forced by "rational" decisions into remaining in their relatively backward state, and the more advanced ones had no desire to be held back so that others could reach their level.

Khrushchev, as it appeared clearly from an article he wrote at the time,[4] intended to proceed rapidly toward real economic integration. This meant centralized authority to control investments and make other basic decisions. Khrushchev saw integration as the only way to use the full resources of the bloc and to stand up to the growing economic power of the West. He talked of a great "world socialist market" which by 1980 would leave the capitalist world far behind. It would presumably be totally self-sufficient, with no need of trade with the West.

Obviously, an integrated economy would have to have a central body with authority. Could that body be a committee representing eight sovereign countries (by 1962 Albania was out but Outer Mongolia was in), each with the right of veto? Or would it have to be a supranational authority that could on economic grounds take decisions ignoring national boundaries, national governments, and national plans, for the greater good of the whole? Such a central body would surely be a Soviet agency. The basic issue of national plans versus integration was posed most sharply in Rumania.

The Strange Case of Rumania

Rumania was one of the less developed of the satellites, with one of the most subservient and least venturesome regimes in the

[4] Nikita S. Khrushchev, "Vital Questions of the Development of the World Socialist System," *World Marxist Review: Problems of Peace and Socialism,* Vol. 5, No. 9, September 1962, pp. 3–180.

bloc. It was exploited ruthlessly by the Soviet Union during the Stalin period. After Stalin's death the worst aspects of that exploitation were changed, and in the late 1950s the Soviets provided Rumania with some industrial plants and installations, especially for the chemical industry. By this time the Rumanian regime, having survived the first wave of de-Stalinization without altering its basic Stalinist mold, began to gain confidence in itself; it achieved one of the highest rates of economic growth in the bloc, and it had available a new generation of qualified young people from the universities and polytechnical schools that made possible new and more ambitious plans for industrialization. In 1959 decisions were taken to press forward rapidly with massive new investments, with the heavy and machine-building industries as the "pivot" for socialist development.

It is interesting that Rumania's new economic plan was set forth at the Third Party Congress in Bucharest in June 1960, the very meeting at which the Soviet-Chinese dispute broke into the open. While the Rumanians were on the Soviet side so far as the main issues of that dispute were concerned, they were not uninfluenced by the Chinese arguments in favor of an "elevated rhythm" of development for the less developed socialist economies enabling them to catch up with the more advanced; like the Chinese, they had plenty of quotations from Lenin to back them up. In any event, the Chinese and Albanian attitudes toward Moscow surely encouraged the Rumanians to try the power of positive thinking. The "Statement" that came out of the ensuing Moscow conference of eighty-one Communist parties in the fall of 1960 included an ardent profession of faith in the equality of all the parties and the sovereignty of Communist states. The principle of sovereign equality, endorsed by both Russians and Chinese, has become the basic text of Rumania's economic policy.

Rumanian plans include a huge steel complex at Galatz which would bring national production to some seven million tons per year, putting Rumania near the level of East Germany, Poland, and Czechoslovakia in that respect. The project has become a symbol of Rumania's aspirations to close the gap with those others and not lag behind in the forward march from socialism to communism, which according to an earlier statement of Khrushchev's all socialist states were to reach more or less at the same time. But at a time of organizing a proper division of labor in the bloc, of marshaling resources for their maximum use, such a project was wholly out of line. Even before Rumania's plans came to C.M.E.A. for review, Moscow had shown its bearish views by offering Soviet technical help and equipment (for sale) only for a smaller steel project and had expressed strong doubts about the usefulness of "universal industrialization" in another small country.

Rumania, meanwhile, had begun to increase its trade with Western Europe. If it could not get needed equipment from the bloc, it would look elsewhere. The following trade statistics [5] are instructive:

	Volume of Rumanian Foreign Trade (*in millions of lei*)				
	1958	*1959*	*1960*	*1961*	*1962*
Total	5,700	6,146	8,189	9,642	10,556
Within the bloc	4,432	4,905	5,981	6,554	7,094
With the free world ..	1,268	1,240	2,208	3,088	3,461

Thus from 1959 to 1962, while trade with the bloc increased by some 45 per cent, that with the free world nearly trebled. And of the bloc trade the Soviet Union's share dropped from 51.5 per cent in 1958 to 40.6 per cent in 1962. The Rumanians found that they could get in the West the equipment they wanted for their new industries, and they discovered it was better than comparable equipment in the East. They had a good bargaining position, especially because of the Soviet-Chinese conflict which they knew how to exploit, and could feel fairly sure that force would not be used against them.

The matter came to a showdown at the C.M.E.A. meeting of December 1962. Rumania was intent on keeping its freedom of action, on not being frozen in a state of permanent underdevelop-

[5] The statistics are taken from the United Nations *Yearbook of International Trade Statistics 1962* (New York: United Nations, 1964), p. 585. The figures have been rounded off and so do not always add up to the total.

ment and inferiority in relation to the more industrialized states of the bloc. The result of the meeting was what the chief Polish delegate called a "creative compromise." It was in fact a defeat for the idea of supranational authority, and thus a defeat for Khrushchev. The Rumanians were not alone, nor were they alone at the next "summit" meeting of Communist Party leaders at Moscow in July 1963. There the final communiqué reaffirmed the sovereignty of all member states and stressed bilateral relations as the best possible basis for the coordination of economic plans. While a C.M.E.A. Bank has been established and some progress made in short-term measures of coordination, the planned advance in real integration has been slowed to a walk, to suit the pace of the most reluctant Eastern European states.

East-West Trade

One cannot be sure at this stage how economic relations between Eastern and Western Europe will develop. If the Common Market becomes an autarchic unit and the C.M.E.A. area does the same, trade between them will dry up except for possible bloc-to-bloc bilateral barter deals which both might on occasion find beneficial. Economic and political factors are obviously interlocked. Whether a drive toward self-sufficiency and the curtailment of trade takes place depends on political decisions in East and West; and the very fact of its taking place, for whatever reasons, would have inevitable political effects. On the other hand, relatively open economic relations and a growth in East-West trade may be supported on one side or the other on political grounds, although the reasons would probably be quite different on the two sides and the results not easily predictable.

Past attitudes on East-West trade may be roughly defined as follows:

1. The United States, since the late 1940s, has seen East-West trade (except for trade in "nonstrategic" items like food and consumer goods) as a means whereby its enemies can strengthen themselves with the help of Western goods and technical information, and therefore as a danger. The Export Control Act of 1949

provides the basic authority for the denial or limitation of exports in the interest of national security. The Battle Act of 1951, which is mainly concerned with controlling trade with the Soviet bloc on the part of other free-world states as well as the United States, gives as the aims of its provisions: "to (1) increase the national strength of the United States and of the cooperating nations; (2) impede the ability of nations threatening the security of the United States to conduct military operations; and (3) to assist the people of the nations under the domination of foreign aggressors to reestablish their freedom." [6] Nations receiving American aid had to embargo the same goods the United States did in the category of arms and other items of primary strategic significance, and also cooperate with the United States in the regulation of other exports to Communist countries, or have their aid cut off.

2. The Western European governments accepted the general American approach, but only partially; they have been decreasingly willing to apply export controls as strict as ours. They are more attracted by the economic benefits of trade with the East and under strong pressure from their own business communities to let them participate in it. Now that most of them are no longer receiving American aid, they are not subject to the same penalties as they were in the 1950s.

3. The Soviet Union has looked on trade with the West as a useful means of getting the capital goods, particularly machinery and machine tools, needed for its economic expansion; hence its continuing clamor for the ending of artificial barriers to such trade.

4. The Eastern European governments, whether from loyalty to Moscow or for reasons of their own, have shared this Soviet view; more recently, some have looked on trade with the West as an alternative source of needed goods and a means of lessening their economic dependence on the Soviet Union.

The statistics on the volume of East-West trade help to explain past developments and also the main considerations affecting future policies. Tables 2 and 3 show the volume of American and

[6] *Mutual Defense Assistance Control Act of 1951*, Public Law 213, 82nd Congress, 1st session, October 26, 1951. See the Administrator's *First Report to Congress*, October 15, 1952, p. 31.

Western European trade with the Soviet Union and the Eastern European states of the bloc for four sample years covering the last decade and a half. Western Europe's trade with the East has increased steadily in the past few years to quite substantial levels, reflecting both the relaxation of controls and the increased desire for trade on both sides. American trade took a sharp drop after the imposition of export controls and has stayed at a very low level, with the one exception of trade with Poland after 1956. Of the $112.6 million in American exports to the bloc in 1958, $104.6 million went to Poland. Of the $125 million in exports in 1962, $94.45 million went to Poland. The proportion of imports from Poland was not so high, but they still averaged about three-quarters of total American imports from all the satellites.

Table 2. United States Trade with the U.S.S.R. and Eastern Europe
(in thousands of dollars)

Year	Exports to U.S.S.R.	Imports from U.S.S.R.	Exports to Eastern Europe	Imports from Eastern Europe
1948	28,002	86,841	95,239	26,298
1954	216	11,929	5,905	30,478
1958	3,422	17,558	109,153	46,015
1962	20,141	16,181	104,995	62,718

Table 3. Western Europe's * Trade with the U.S.S.R. and Eastern Europe
(in thousands of dollars)

Year	Exports to U.S.S.R.	Imports from U.S.S.R.	Exports to Eastern Europe	Imports from Eastern Europe
1948	183,000	304,800	489,500	730,900
1952	384,300	383,900	517,500	616,400
1958	594,600	704,100	1,012,500	1,082,900
1962	1,057,900	1,168,600	1,543,700	1,579,400

SOURCE for Tables 2 and 3: *Mutual Defense Assistance Control Act of 1951, Reports of the Administrator to Congress* (Washington, D.C.: Government Printing Office). Data adapted from 7th Report, 1955, Tables 3C–3F, pp. 74–77; 13th Report, 1960, Tables 2A–2C, 5A, pp. 39–42, 49; and 16th Report, 1963, Tables 3A–3D, 6A, pp. 53–61, 70. Totals in Table 3 are rounded off and should be regarded as approximate.

*Includes Finland (except reparation deliveries) and Greece but not Turkey or Yugoslavia.

Western Europe's trade with the bloc is clearly expanding rapidly. Political and economic factors, in the light of the relative relaxation in the cold war, have built up pressure against the system of trade controls agreed upon by the NATO countries and kept under review by a Coordinating Committee sitting in Paris. Relations among the allies, principally between the European countries and the United States, have been subjected to considerable strain as the result of disagreements over what exports to control and precisely how to control them. The United States was often in a position of having to accept changes in the lists of banned or restricted goods if it did not wish to see its partners go their own way and thus destroy the whole system. Washington did not relax its own export controls to any appreciable extent, but the general trend toward lowering the barriers was bound to bring pressure on the part of American business to be able to share in trade with the Soviet bloc on an equal basis with European competitors.

It is not possible to determine how much of a contribution goods like copper wire or steel pipe obtained from the West by Communist countries will actually make to Soviet military potential endangering the United States. It is probably marginal, considering the Soviet Union's virtual self-sufficiency and its concentration of its own resources on building military power. There is an additional reason put forward as justification for tight trade controls: that any imports of needed goods from the West help the Soviet and satellite regimes to make their system succeed, and that the West has no interest in providing such help. That argument applies to export of food, which the United States has been willing to send both to Eastern Europe and to the U.S.S.R. itself, as well as of machinery and other strategic goods, for food imports relieve the Communists of paying the full penalty for the failure of their own agricultural system. On the other side it is argued that, in addition to economic gains for the West, an expanding East-West trade will increase the Soviet leadership's stake in peaceful coexistence and emphasize its interest in "goulash communism" as opposed to world revolution — in short, that fat Communists will be less dangerous to the West than skinny Communists.

These issues should be and will be debated at length within Western countries and among them. They are, it should be noted, concerned with overall policy toward the bloc as a whole. They take no account of the centrifugal forces now at work in Eastern Europe or of the possible usefulness of Western policies which make distinctions among the various Communist states. As can be seen from the statistics, the United States has in fact made such a distinction in the case of Poland. Poland was not exempted from the system of controls, but after 1956 it received credits for the purchase of American goods, was permitted to buy American grain and cotton for Polish currency, and was granted most-favored-nation treatment (in 1960). In 1964, following negotiations with Rumania, the United States eased the licensing procedures for exports to that country and opened the way for commercial credits, moves which were definitely related to Rumania's current differences with the Soviet Union. Yugoslavia, while still a Communist state after 1948, was given exemptions from the export control system and not regarded as a member of the bloc at all.

Because Western Europe's trade with Eastern Europe is so much greater than ours, the trends in the exchanges between the two parts of Europe are especially important in considering the advantages and disadvantages to both sides and the relation of trade to political aims. For Western Europe, trade with Eastern Europe (excluding the U.S.S.R.) is but a fraction of its total world trade. In 1960 and 1961 the average percentage was roughly 2.6. For the satellite states, on the other hand, 21 per cent of their exports went to Western Europe in those years and 18 per cent of their imports came from there. The implication is that the trade is more important to Eastern than to Western Europe and that the greater bargaining power lies with the West.

Eastern Europe's trade with the West, moreover, has been increasing during the very years that C.M.E.A. has been engaged in loud talk and feverish activity directed to the socialist division of labor and the economic integration of the bloc (see Table 1). The fact is that the Eastern European countries, at this stage of their development and for some time in the future, cannot get from the Soviet Union or from each other all that they need to build their economies in the way they desire. Only through exports to the West or credits can they get the free currency they must have to buy in world markets; only in the West can they get the kinds of capital equipment they need.

The policy aspects of this situation for the West are related to varying assumptions and to varying interpretations which may be placed upon what is happening and will happen in Eastern Europe. Trade with the West will undoubtedly help the regimes solve their economic problems. Inability to trade will compound the problems. Some in the West believe that there is no advantage to be found in making life easier for a Communist regime allied to the Soviet Union; on that assumption, trade should be cut down or cut off or at least used as a means of getting political concessions. Others — and this is the general view of the Western European governments — believe that it is advantageous to build up strong ties of trade, to give the Eastern European states a choice and not drive them back into total dependence on the Soviet Union, and to reknit the ties that drew the two halves of Europe together before the advent of Soviet domination.

In today's atmosphere of relative détente it would be difficult to cut down, on political grounds, Western Europe's trade with Eastern Europe. Business interests and general economic considerations tend to support the political reasons given for increasing trade. For the United States there is a real question whether trying to maintain Western agreement on even the present level of export controls is worth the continued bickering and disunity it has brought into relations among the NATO allies.

IV POLAND: A SPECIAL CASE WITHIN THE BLOC

P OLAND'S position in the Soviet bloc and its relations with the West are determined more by geography than by ideology. A small nation located between the German and Russian giants and with no natural defenses, the Poles throughout history have had to wage fierce struggles to maintain their national existence. Although their nation was wiped off the map of Europe for a century and a quarter, they and the cause of Polish independence survived by virtue of their intense nationalism and the world's awareness of it. The restored Poland of the interwar period essayed a role beyond its powers and failed to use wisely the room for maneuver it had between Germany and Russia; it had little enough anyway, once Hitler was able to rearm Germany and the League of Nations' system of collective security proved its impotence. Whether Polish independence could have survived an arrangement with Stalin in 1939 is an arguable question; at any rate, it did not long survive the Polish government's refusal to come to terms with Russia. The British guarantee could not prevent the fourth partition of Poland which Hitler and Stalin proceeded to carry out.

From the Soviet standpoint, Poland's location is crucial to Soviet security. When considering during the war the shape of postwar Europe, Stalin wished to make sure that Poland would never regain the eastern territories which the Soviet Union had annexed following the pact with Hitler in 1939, that Poland would never again serve as an avenue for a German invasion, and that Poland would not fall into the hands of a government hostile to the Soviet Union. For all these reasons he insisted on the Curzon Line as Poland's eastern frontier and on blocking any return of the government-in-exile to Poland. To make the territorial losses in the east easier for the Polish people, and for a pro-Soviet regime, he advocated pushing the western frontier much further to the west at the expense of Germany. To prepare the way for a friendly regime, he broke relations with the government-in-exile in 1943 and organized on Soviet soil a group that took over governing authority in the wake of the Soviet army as it marched across Poland in 1944 and 1945.

These designs of Stalin largely determined the postwar settlement. The Western powers finally accepted what was substantially the Curzon Line in the east after some halfhearted attempts to save something more for Poland. They accepted the Oder-Neisse line in the west on a provisional and *de facto* basis, reserving the final determination of the frontier for the peace settlement. They tried to preserve for the Polish people a free choice of regime, but in the end they recognized a government in which the Communists held the whip hand and were in a position to eliminate all rivals and to manage all subsequent elections. This "People's Poland," then, was the Soviet Union's shield against a revived Germany, against the anti-Soviet feeling of the Polish people, and against any machinations of the Western powers.

How did the settlement serve Polish, as opposed to Soviet, interests? There was no doubt that the great majority of Poles, Communist and non-Communist, hated and feared Germany and saw the need for protection against a German campaign to regain the lost territories. They were insistent on keeping those territories, which they regarded as vital to Poland's very existence. And they were concerned, though the Communist regime's actions gave little evidence of it, with safeguarding the nation against *both* Germany and Russia. The new western lands were, incidentally, more valuable though less extensive than those lost to the Soviet Union in the east. The Polish people, however, were not so grateful for their gains that they did not resent bitterly the imposition of a Communist regime and the loss of all but the appearance of their own independent state. Their new top leaders, with few exceptions, were individuals who had arrived in the baggage train of the Soviet army and were Soviet agents rather than Polish patriots. The prewar leaders of the Polish Communist Party, who had also followed a Soviet rather than a Polish line, had nevertheless been wiped out in the Stalinist purge of the late 1930s.

There was one element in the Communist leadership, however, that had a sharp consciousness of the need to take account of interests that were Polish. Wladyslaw Gomulka, who spent the war years as a resistance leader within Poland, was convinced from the start that Polish Communists, if they were to have any chance of lasting success, had to pay heed to national interest and popular feelings. In 1947 he wrote that "we have chosen our own Polish road to development." For that reason he and his friends were vulnerable when the Yugoslav defection in 1948 set Stalin off on a witch hunt for Titoists in every satellite state. Gomulka was not hard to identify as a Titoist. He had not accepted Stalin's view on how to handle Tito and was not permitted to attend the Bucharest meeting of the Cominform at which the resolution condemning the Yugoslav leadership was adopted. Although one of the top leaders of his party, he was censured by its central committee for his defense of Tito and his tendencies toward "bourgeois nationalism." It took some time for Bierut and the other Stalinists in the party to deprive him of his governmental and party posts, but in 1951 he was finally arrested and imprisoned. Poland, unlike other satellites, had no bloody purge. Gomulka was never brought to trial, probably because he could not be counted on to confess the crimes charged to him and could say much that was uncomfortable for his accusers. For whatever Polish or Soviet reasons, he was not executed, and languished in jail until his hour of triumph struck in 1956.

The End of the Stalinist Regime

During Stalin's later years and for some time after his death the Communist regime in Warsaw clamped an iron hand on Poland.

Politically, the dictatorship of the party, supported by the security police, grew ever more arbitrary and absolute. Economically, the theorists and practitioners of centralized planning and forced development of heavy industry paid scant attention to the needs of the people or even to some of the elementary laws of economics. Intellectual life was stifled by censorship. Backing up the power of the regime was the directing influence of the Soviet Union, most vividly symbolized by the presence of a Soviet marshal, Konstantin Rokossovsky, in the cabinet as minister of defense. Soviet troops occupied the country. The high posts in the Polish armed forces were held by Soviet officers; the secret police served as an instrument of Soviet power; the Polish administration and party organizations were honeycombed with Soviet agents.

Then, about two years after the death of Stalin, the system showed signs of cracking. Defections from the secret police exposed its horrifying record. The economic machinery began to creak and break down. A daring new literature appeared and, surprisingly, was not totally suppressed. The new Soviet leaders, increasingly skeptical of the capacity of Poland's top Communists to cope with the new problems of the post-Stalin period, opened their minds to the possibility of sacrificing some of them. Popular pressure against the regime, though without legal means of open expression, was nevertheless felt both in Warsaw and in Moscow. The Poznan strike and riots in June 1956 showed that the workers were capable of violence against the regime. There had to be a new leadership in the party and some change in policies or the regime itself might collapse in the face of mass disaffection.

The Polish October and the Gomulka Regime

Gomulka's return to the position of leader of the Polish Workers' Party provoked, or coincided with, a crisis in Soviet-Polish relations. As we have noted, the Soviet leaders in effect left to the new Gomulka regime authority to run Polish internal affairs in its own way. But they sought and obtained assurance that Poland would remain within the bloc. The agreement on the stationing of Soviet forces in Poland contained strict and precise limitations, obvious concessions to the Poles, but the vital fact was that the Soviet troops remained. After a short period that seemed to presage a more independent foreign policy, including some divergence on the Hungarian question and Poland's absence from a meeting of Soviet and Eastern European leaders at Budapest, by 1958 Gomulka had come fully into line with Moscow on all international questions. He did ask for American financial aid and received it, year after year, but whether or not he did so against Soviet wishes in the first instance, Khrushchev came to accept it as no threat to Poland's position as a member of the bloc.

On the domestic front the Gomulka regime first put through some rather drastic changes. They included allowing the dissolution of the collective farms, with the result that rural Poland again became almost wholly a land of independent peasant proprietors; removal of the worst aspects of the police terror; a new relationship with the Catholic Church which permitted the latter to carry on its activities with much less interference and persecution than before and even to give religious instruction in the public schools (a privilege later taken away); a more meaningful role for the national parliament and other political institutions; some decentralization of economic organization and experimentation with workers' councils; and a greater freedom of academic, literary, and artistic expression that made Poland a unique case within the Soviet bloc.

All these measures were in the nature of concessions to the people. They enabled the regime to keep the necessary minimum of popular support while it tackled its own difficult problems and tried to stabilize its position both at home and in foreign relations. Its relations with the Church, in particular, were in effect a political compromise which enabled them to live with each other despite the incompatibility of their respective philosophies.

As the years passed, however, the Gomulka regime began to encroach on many of the gains of the Polish October. As the Communist leaders rebuilt their party, which had demonstrated its lack of popular support in 1956, they began to harass the Church more and to tighten their grip on the people. Economic decentralization never went very far, and the workers' councils were emasculated through party control. Particularly in the realm of freedom of expression, the rather euphoric atmosphere of 1956 and early 1957, when revisionism and liberalism were the inspiration of many intellectuals and some political leaders, began to recede under pressure from the authorities. From the time of the suppression of the student publication *Po Prostu* in 1957 and the riots that accompanied it, the tide of free expression ebbed. Particularly among the youth there was widespread disillusionment and a tendency to reject all ideology and concern with political matters. Nevertheless, in spite of the retreat, Poland remained quite different from the rest of Eastern Europe. Its relative freedom both from Soviet control and from full-fledged totalitarianism at home was known to the ruling regimes and to many of the inhabitants of the other states. In recent years, as the more rigid patterns in some of those states have begun to crack, the contrast is not nearly so sharp; yet Poland's influence as the example and pace setter after 1956 should not be underestimated.

The Polish Workers' (Communist) Party has within it a number of factions, ranging from remnants of the liberals and revisionists to those who would like to restore something like the tough police state of the Stalin period. The distinctions are anything but clearcut, however; those who are strongly nationalist are not necessarily the most liberal. Gomulka has followed a middle course, always keeping control in his own hands. Although he has made no basic change in political and economic policies, that course has tended more and more in the direction of tight control. The intellectuals are restive and have been moved to protest. The Catholic Church, while not under frontal attack, has been subjected to further harrying. Gomulka has been steadily losing the popularity he won with the Polish people for the role he played in 1956. They realize, however, that there is no better alternative in sight.

Poland's Foreign Relations

It is an oversimplification to say that Poland is allowed to enjoy internal autonomy in exchange for following the Kremlin line in matters of foreign policy. It is even less accurate to attribute Gomulka's foreign policy to ideological solidarity with Moscow, although that is an element in it. The fact is, as has already been pointed out, that the vital strategic interests of both the Soviet Union and Poland combine to set narrow limits on Poland's role in international affairs.

For the Soviet Union, Poland is strategically the most important of all the countries of the Soviet European bloc. Defensively, control of Poland makes it possible to guard against the building up of hostile power on the Soviet western frontier and helps to block any eastward move by Germany or other powers backing Germany. Offensively, it holds open the road to Germany and Central Europe; it enables the Soviet Union to hold on to East Germany and to play for control of the whole of Germany, which Soviet leaders since Lenin have regarded as the key to Europe.

Poland's perspective is naturally different, but fear of a revived and aggressive Germany is even stronger in Polish than in Soviet thinking because of the differences in size and strength. Association with Russia against Germany is therefore natural for Poland and is in fact a current in Polish thought that long predates the advent of a Communist regime.[1] Although officially Poland is content with the attitude of the East German regime, which recognizes the Oder-Neisse line, the Poles are basically distrustful of all Germans and fear the reunification of Germany under any auspices, Western or Soviet, democratic or Communist.

While depending on Russia, Poland has had to be on guard against being swallowed up by its huge eastern neighbor. This we have seen to be a common concern of the Gomulka regime and of Polish leaders of an earlier day. Here Gomulka is obviously relying on the reluctance of the Soviet leadership to push Poland too far. That was a vital factor in his relationship with Khrushchev, which rested on a real measure of mutual confidence despite the fact that at their first dramatic encounter in October 1956 he defied the So-

[1] This is a major point of Adam Bromke's article "Communism and Nationalism in Poland," *Foreign Affairs*, Vol. 40 (July 1962), pp. 635–43, which formed a part of the original paper prepared for the Wingspread conference.

viet leader to his face. Khrushchev came to respect him more than the other Communist leaders of Eastern Europe and to engage in genuine consultation with him. Gomulka, too, was the first foreign Communist leader with whom Khrushchev's successors conferred, and on Polish soil at that, after removing their chief from the seats of power. Although Soviet troops remain in Poland, the Warsaw regime apparently feels that the measure of independence Poland has gained could not be taken away by Moscow except at the cost of destruction of the whole edifice of "voluntary cooperation" which has been built as a substitute for the imperial structure that existed under Stalin.

Poland has thus relied on the trend toward polycentrism in the Soviet bloc as a means of consolidating and gradually increasing the amount of independence it can enjoy. It seeks to assure its national interests within the bloc rather than in any risky attempt to withdraw from it. At the same time it hopes to use the changing relationships between East and West as a means of gaining certain international guarantees for its position and of establishing ties with the West, ties that will counterbalance in some degree its dependence on the Soviet Union and make possible a greater flexibility and bargaining power in Polish foreign policy. That is part of the motivation for the Rapacki Plan and other proposals for internationally agreed upon disengagement and arms limitation, the logical end result of which might be a position of neutrality something like that of Finland. It also explains, in part, Poland's desire to increase and improve economic and cultural relations with the Western nations.

Poland has, after all, a long tradition of close association with the West over many centuries. It has, in addition, a special tie with the United States resulting from the presence here of several million Americans of Polish descent. Since 1956 Poland has opened its doors to representatives of Western countries and has permitted thousands of its own citizens to visit Western Europe and the United States. It has entered into regular programs of cultural exchange. It has sought to increase trade with the West and has received financial and economic aid annually from the United

States in the form of loans and purchases of American surplus agricultural products for Polish currency. While the cultivation of ties with the West carries certain risks for the Communist regime, because it may encourage anti-Communist trends among the Polish population, Gomulka and his colleagues have felt able to control such risks and thus far have succeeded in doing so.

Let us now look at the situation from the specific standpoint of the interests and policies of the United States. A policy of continuing aid to Poland has been followed ever since 1957 by the Eisenhower, Kennedy, and Johnson administrations. It has been followed in the face of much anti-American propaganda on the part of the Warsaw regime and of Gomulka's clear intention to adhere to the Soviet position on Germany and other issues of East-West relations. It has been followed, also, in the face of a certain amount of opposition in the United States Congress, evident in the stops and starts on the question of trade. In 1951, as a cold war measure, the United States withdrew all trade concessions previously made to states which were then in the Soviet bloc, including Poland. In 1960 most-favored-nation treatment was restored to Poland. Then in 1962 the Congress withdrew it again and only restored it again in 1963 after considerable pushing on the part of the administration.[2] Congress struck another blow in 1964, cutting off Poland's purchases of surplus farm products for Polish currency as of the end of that year. American policy, nevertheless, continues to be based on the idea that only by active measures to foster trade and cultural relations can Western influence be exerted, and that special treatment of Poland, which has asserted a position of its own within the Soviet bloc, is bound to have favorable repercussions elsewhere in the Communist world.

As in the case of Yugoslavia, the direct effect of such a policy is impossible to measure. In any event, the desired results appear to be taking place, however one chooses to assess the relative contributions of their various causes.

[2] See Milorad M. Drachkovitch, *United States Aid to Yugoslavia and Poland: Analysis of a Controversy* (Washington, D.C.: American Enterprise Institute, 1963), for a critique of both sides of the question.

V *YUGOSLAVIA: A SPECIAL CASE OUTSIDE THE BLOC*

IN THE past few years Yugoslavia has had ample reason to be reminded that while it may be a prominent leader of the nonaligned group, it is also a small Balkan country whose fate depends in large measure on what happens beyond its borders and beyond its control. In Washington, the United States Congress has on occasion singled out Yugoslavia as a special target of its displeasure. The Trade Expansion Act of 1962 withdrew most-favored-nation treatment from Yugoslav goods, and only the efforts of the administration and a slim majority in the Senate kept in the foreign aid bill the provision permitting economic assistance. In the nations of Western Europe, where attention is fixed on the shape of the new European community, Yugoslav concerns have encountered little more than frosty indifference, although Italy has been friendly. From the other side of the world comes the continuing barrage of Chinese Communist invective against "Titoist revisionism." From Moscow, in contrast, the Yugoslavs have heard some conciliatory noises, but they were scarcely heartened by Khrushchev's efforts, through the Council for Mutual Economic Assistance, to make the Eastern bloc more exclusive and self-contained than ever. At home, meanwhile, Tito and his colleagues have faced manifold troubles largely of their own making. If they did not call it a crisis, it had all the earmarks of one, in which difficulties on the economic side were accompanied by an evident political malaise.

All these events have combined to raise questions about Yugoslav foreign policy at a time when it seemed to have attained a certain stability. The world has long since become accustomed to Yugoslavia's insistence on full national independence as the foundation stone of its international position. The Soviet Union has come to accept, although not always with good grace, Tito's maintenance of important economic ties with the West, ties which were crucial to his country's survival in the struggle against Soviet pressures during the Stalin era and which still serve both Yugoslav and Western interests. The West, in turn, has accepted Tito's self-righteous neutralism, with some reservations concerning the unneutral way in which, on occasion, it works out in practice. It has accepted as well, though not without feeling uneasy about it, his endeavors to find a new and "normal" basis for relations with the Soviet Union over the period of alternating reconciliation and mutual denunciation which began with Khrushchev's visit to Belgrade in 1955. Western aid in one form or another, particularly American aid, has continued to go to Yugoslavia ever since 1949.

Have recent events called into question these fixed points of Yugoslav policy, and therefore of Western policies based on them? Does the more conciliatory attitude toward Tito which Khrushchev espoused as the conflict with China deepened hold out prospects for more solid and lasting Yugoslav cooperation with Moscow? Has Tito's practice of positive neutralism brought the country to a new and promising position in world affairs, or to a dead end? Thus far there has been no drastic change on Yugoslavia's part, though the increasing cordiality in relations with the Soviet Union and other Communist states in Eastern Europe (except Albania) is unmistakable. But Tito and his colleagues still face some hard choices, which compel a reassessment of where the country stands.

Before turning to Yugoslavia's dilemmas in foreign policy we must consider the internal situation, for the two are intimately connected.

The Yugoslav Economy

The country's economic plight is not a happy one. Agriculture, since the bumper crops of 1959, has been a keen disappointment.

Neither new investments in fertilizers, Italian-type wheat, and hybrid corn nor the indefinite postponement of collectivization and the easing of pressure on the peasants have brought production to a constant annual level that enables the country to feed itself. The weather in the last few years has struck cruel blows. It would seem to be about time to include bad weather in the calculus of hopes and plans for agricultural production; the good year has become the exception, not the rule.

In industry there is uncertainty, as the regime has sought the best combination of planning and use of the free market. In some ways, it now appears, the market has been a little too free. Individual firms and local governments have misdirected investment. Needed foreign exchange has been wasted on nonessential imports. Workers' councils have distributed profits in bonuses for themselves at the expense of needed investment. Managers of enterprises have accumulated considerable personal wealth. Consumption has gone up, as have prices and wages, while productivity by contrast has not consistently kept pace. On the surface, Yugoslavia looks more prosperous each year. The greater variety and quality of clothing and the growing number of private automobiles provide evidence apparent to everyone. But some of Yugoslavia's economists have been asking embarrassing questions about uneconomic investment, low productivity of labor, and the limitations of the planning system.

The international balance of payments problem has continued to plague the country and perpetuate its dependence on foreign aid and credits. Try as it did, Yugoslavia seemed to make no dent in its trade deficit. If exports went up, imports went up also. For 1961, the adverse balance was a sobering $167 million (not counting imports of American agricultural surplus paid for in dinars), and the foreign debt, in the neighborhood of $800 million, presented a heavy repayment burden over the next few years. For 1962 the adverse trade balance was $199 million; for 1963, $269 million. Exports have improved but without bringing any real change in the situation. The bold exchange-rate reform introduced in 1961, sound as it was in conception, made the situation all the more difficult when the supporting credits from the International Monetary Fund and other sources proved less helpful than was hoped and the controls necessary to conserve foreign exchange were not established.

By the spring of 1962 it was apparent that the Yugoslav economic experiment had produced no magic formula for success; that the country had not reached the point of self-sustaining growth; that, indeed, it might be heading for serious trouble. President Tito, sounding the alarm in an important speech at Split in May 1962, said that corrective measures would be taken, and that those who had waxed fat at public expense — the traders, plant directors, and others who had achieved prominence as conspicuous consumers — would be dealt with according to their deserts. His speech, which had in it a note of desperation, indirectly pointed up the political aspect of the crisis. The remedies to be applied were political as well as economic. The people, and especially the Communists, should revive the old spirit and the old discipline, so that things might be set right. If the leaders did not envisage an abandonment of the whole free-market side of the system and a return to centralized planning and the tight party dictatorship of the old days — and it was soon made clear that they did not — the emphasis on new commissions and shifting of personnel, on party control and party discipline, showed the color of Tito's thinking. But the regime had no clear answers. For the next two years the economists argued the merits of centralization and decentralization, and the party straddled the issue.

During the past decade Tito's own reforms have greatly changed the character of Yugoslav society, perhaps more than he himself realizes or can control. At any rate, party spirit will not solve the problems of an economy far more complex than that of 1948, and the role of the party itself has changed both in theory and in fact.

Changing Political Institutions

At its Sixth Congress, held in 1952, the Communist Party of Yugoslavia changed its name and its mission. As the League of Communists, its job was to be primarily one of education, guidance, and example rather than of direction and control. No one was under any illusion concerning the continuing central role of the party. Yet the fact that, under the stress of conflict with the Soviet Union and in the search for "true" forms of Leninism, the leaders were publicly referring to the gradual withering away of the state *and of the party* could not but have its effect on the attitudes both of party members and of the population in general. Despite uncertainty and confusion over the party's role in the years which followed, the Seventh Congress, held in 1958, confirmed the basic tenets of the Sixth. Today the party is still the ultimate authority, as the pronouncements of its Central Committee have made clear. The new constitution of 1963 calls it "the fundamental initiator of political activity." It can still use arbitrary police power, and sometimes does. It does not tolerate political opposition or permit talk of a two-party system, as Milovan Djilas can testify. But it is not what it was.

The rise of a new generation is a part of this picture. As the changes of the past dozen years have taken hold, new loyalties and new ambitions have motivated Yugoslavia's bright young men. The economic system and political institutions have become more complex. There has been much experimentation, some of it under the influence of ideas coming in through the doors the regime has opened to the non-Communist world. The cement that held the leadership together — the common experience in the prewar revolutionary movement, in the partisan military struggle, and in the absorbing task of establishing socialism and then defending it against outside threats and pressures — is no longer as binding as it once was. Many of the old partisans are not equal to the different challenges of a new day. Some have only one claim to leadership — the fact that they were partisans — and are neither sympathetic to the new reforms nor qualified to administer them. As the party relaxed the grip of its police power, it did not gain a compensating authority in public prestige. Many party men, as prosperity grew, were comporting themselves like members of the "new class" described by Djilas. Factionalism, drawing on personal rivalries and the old antagonism between nationalities and fed by uncertainty where the regime was going, appeared within the party ranks.

Somewhere along the line the Tito regime, consciously or unconsciously, took a basic decision on what it was trying to do, namely to build pragmatically a system that would produce goods for the people and provide some measure of economic self-management and political responsibility. Institutions of "social self-government and socialist democracy," such as the workers' councils and the local communes, were gradually brought into being and strengthened over the years; they are enshrined in the new constitution. The party organs are still very much in the picture, but the fact remains that these other institutions are acquiring a life of their own.

The new institutions have a Marxist label. They are part of the "building of socialism." But the young men and women who have grown up with this system have been more interested in making it work than in party loyalty, party discipline, or even party membership. They are concerned with getting jobs that challenge them and reward them; with such matters as science and its practical application, economics, public administration, and even artistic expression, rather than with the theory of transition from socialism to communism or the search for a Leninist rationale for what they are doing. They are beginning to attain governmental posts of some importance, though not yet the top positions. As the years go by, barring some wholesale purge or reversion to the past which could conceivably accompany a crisis over the succession to Tito, they are likely to grow in importance.

Between East and West

These political trends, often under the surface and not immediately evident, are bound to affect the present leaders' attempts to cope with economic and other domestic difficulties. Will they also affect Yugoslavia's international position, immediately or in the long run? Differences that exist on internal policy — centralization versus decentralization, discipline versus liberalization, ideology versus pragmatism — have found some parallel in conflicting or ambivalent attitudes on foreign policy.

There is no doubt that Yugoslavia has greatly benefited by Western assistance in maintaining its independence and in building its own version of socialism. There is no doubt either that bitterness against the West today is real, at least so far as those in positions of power are concerned. Yugoslav officials ask why the United States follows no consistent policy toward their country, why it overlooks the fundamental principles of Yugoslavia's position and petulantly criticizes neutralism or the Yugoslav voting record in the United Nations, why it insists on waging cold war against Yugoslavia as it does against the Soviet bloc. They are incensed over the lack of appreciation of their position evident in the acts of the United States Congress and its committees, but without giving much consideration to the Yugoslav regime's own share of the responsibility for American attitudes that are reflected in congressional acts and speeches. On both sides it appears that publicly expressed hostility and misunderstanding have been permitted to becloud the real interests of the two countries.

The great bugbear haunting the Yugoslavs is not America and the possible loss of American economic aid, but the European Common Market and what its mere existence will mean to Yugoslavia. As the Common Market lowers its internal tariffs, outsiders feel the pinch. Yugoslavia has to have markets for its agricultural products in Western Europe, particularly in Italy and Germany, if it is to obtain necessary imports of capital goods and pay its debts. It needs them during the critical period ahead while it attempts to broaden the base of its exports. Some countries of the Common Market have shown a disposition to make adjustments; but with their attention fixed on much broader issues, they seem only marginally concerned with Yugoslavia's plight. If countries like Greece and Austria have trouble in getting terms which meet their needs, the Yugoslavs can hardly be optimistic about the consideration that is going to be given to theirs. They also fear the political implications of the Common Market; if Western Europe becomes a great new world power, Yugoslavia may be squeezed between it and the Soviet bloc with slight chance of having any influence on either one.

Belgrade clings to its alignment with the nonaligned. This has been a useful connection politically, enabling Tito to play on the world stage a role which the size and resources of his country would not otherwise justify. But the conference of unaligned states at Cairo in July 1962 demonstrated, if any demonstration was necessary, that from the economic standpoint the nonaligned countries could provide neither a substitute for ties with the nations of the Common Market nor a serious means of bringing them to terms. Where the Belgrade "summit" conference of 1961 produced a good deal of sound and fury, and Tito's speech there seemed deliberately calculated to please the East even if it annoyed the West, the more modest meeting at Cairo showed a chastened sense of the realities and a willingness to negotiate seriously with the West. That practical approach was still evident in the Yugoslav positions at the second "summit" conference at Cairo in 1964.

Yugoslav officials frankly say that if they do not get understanding and help from the West they must perforce look in the other direction, purely as a matter of economic necessity. A new long-term agreement for expanded trade with the U.S.S.R., concluded in July 1962, bears witness to the seriousness of the attempt to build up trade with the Soviet bloc. They would welcome loans and look to Moscow to renew credits of some $300 million that were suspended for political reasons in 1958. Yet they know that trade with the bloc will be no more than a partial answer to their problem (in 1963 it was still only 25 per cent of total trade), and credits would be of limited value since what Yugoslavia needs above all is free exchange, not loans tied to Soviet or satellite exports. And Yugoslav "businessmen," those who actually run the enterprises, much prefer German and other Western goods for obvious reasons. A really sharp reorientation of trade from West to East is not possible without causing chaos in the economy for at least a year.

Delegations of one kind or another have been plying back and forth between Belgrade and Moscow. They reached the highest

level with the visit of Brezhnev (then titular head of state) to Yugoslavia in the autumn of 1962, Tito's trip to the Soviet Union in December, and Khrushchev's "vacation" in Yugoslavia the following
summer. But how far can the rapprochement go beyond some
increase in trade? Yugoslavia has now been permitted to be associated with some of the activities of the Council for Mutual Economic Assistance, a rough parallel to the observer status it has in
the West's Organization for Economic Cooperation and Development. What Tito wants is to learn what is going on and how Yugoslavia may profit by it, not a commitment to coordinate economic
plans with those of the bloc, involving a loss of the power of independent decision.

Does the prospect of more and closer economic relations with
the East represent a danger to Yugoslavia's independence? Yugoslav leaders say no: first, because they have no intention of taking
any gamble with that independence; second, because they are confident that the Soviet leadership, having finally learned the lesson
that should have been learned years ago, now realizes Yugoslavia
would never accept satellite status. Khrushchev won his fight with
the Stalinists at home, so runs the argument; he repudiated Stalinism in his relations with other countries and stood his ground
against the Stalinist doctrines and policies of Peking; his heirs are
therefore ready for normal state relations and increased economic
cooperation with socialist Yugoslavia. Yugoslav leaders were grati-
fied when Khrushchev stretched out the hand of friendship to
them. It showed courage, they say, for him to defend Yugoslavia
as a socialist state against Chinese charges that Tito was restoring
capitalism. It seemed to confirm their view that rapprochement
was possible on their terms, not on the basis of outworn Stalinist
concepts of domination. They hope that Khrushchev's successors,
to placate China or for any other reasons, will not alter basically
his policy toward Yugoslavia.

One may find such a view of Soviet intentions to be quite naive
without concluding at the same time that Tito is likely to put his
head in a Soviet noose. He and his colleagues have personally experienced both the struggle with Stalin and the ups and downs of

Yugoslav-Soviet relations since his death: the understandings that turned out to be misunderstandings, the reconciliations followed by denunciations, and the bitterness of the still unsolved doctrinal disputes over revisionism and separate roads to socialism. At present the atmosphere is one of friendliness and cooperation. The trend is up rather than down. But the basic pattern of the past ten years is not likely to change. The Yugoslavs have resisted Soviet pressure for total solidarity on major international questions. They never accepted the "troika" proposal for the United Nations; even on Germany they have not endorsed the Soviet position in its entirety. The differences which remain over party programs and over the interpretation of Marxist terms reflect in reality a conflict of national policies and national interests. Whatever line Khrushchev's successors may take, the Yugoslavs are not likely to become so fascinated by the lure of economic help from Russia or by the mirage of fraternal socialist collaboration that they forget those interests. But precisely what they decide to do about the immediate choices before them depends on how they judge the prospects in the West as well as in the East.

Yugoslavia is faced with a situation of great difficulty. If the European Common Market has not shown an inclination to make notable concessions to help Yugoslavia, neither is the Soviet bloc, which has many prior demands on its resources, likely to offer any great benefits just to help Tito make revisionism work. Yugoslavia's role as a member of neither bloc and a suppliant to both seems less promising than at any time since Tito chose his middle course. There is an urgency in the need for more durable relationships, above all with the West.

From the Western viewpoint, some will say that the Yugoslavs made their bed and whether they find it comfortable or not is their own affair. They have had enormous help from the West since their break with Stalin in 1948. The United States provided, up to the end of 1961, over $2 billion in military and economic aid, but still finds Yugoslavia unable to meet its international payments deficit and having to ask, as before, for American food shipments and other help. When these economic facts are seen as part of a general picture which includes Tito's present tactical turn toward the East and his stand on many international issues in direct opposition to the policy of the United States, it is hardly surprising that many American congressmen, including some who can see a difference between Yugoslav and Soviet Communists, are reluctant to provide further assistance.

It is, of course, unwise to determine policy on the basis of disillusionment or spite. But it is in every way proper to re-evaluate the policy which started as a series of emergency measures "to keep Tito afloat" and came to be a regular and consistent effort to support Yugoslavia's independent effort to attain economic stability and progress. That policy has already been reappraised several times, generally under the stress of some new shock administered by Tito himself, and it has shown remarkable staying power. It has been kept in effect, with variations, under all administrations from Truman to Johnson. In judging it in the light of Yugoslavia's present and possible future course, we shall be wise to keep in mind what can reasonably be anticipated in the way of results, and what cannot.

Experience has taught us not to expect too much in tangible returns for our assistance. Western aid and good will have not drawn Yugoslavia into association with NATO — that was clear by 1953 when Tito halted certain tentative steps taken toward cooperation in military planning — nor with its Balkan neighbors, despite the Balkan Alliance which was concluded with Greece and Turkey in 1954 but soon fell into a state of desuetude. They have not brought Yugoslav support on issues concerning Africa, colonialism, disarmament, or Germany, on which Belgrade's policy, though independently reached, has run closer to that of Moscow. Nor has Western aid to Tito had striking results in promoting disruption within the Soviet bloc, although here cause and effect are very difficult to measure.

As we look at the situation in Eastern Europe today, it is at least questionable whether the contrast and competition between Yugoslavia with its freer institutions and the Soviet satellites with their centralized structure on the Soviet model have any sharp meaning.

A few years ago the Yugoslav system seemed to be on top of the wave, clearly doing more for its people and making better economic progress than was being accomplished in the neighboring countries to the east. Today the Yugoslavs are having their problems, while some of the others are not doing badly at all. Rumania, sporting an air of confidence and claiming a better than 15 per cent annual rate of increase in industrial production based largely on new industries like petrochemicals well suited to its resources, has surprised even its own leaders by its progress. Hungary also is doing quite well, thanks largely to the considerable Soviet economic assistance extended to the Kádár regime following the suppression of the revolt of 1956, and to the attitudes of relative tolerance prevailing between the regime and the people. Kádár has finally taken action against the more notorious of those identified with the hated Rákosi regime, and seems intent on winning at least passive support from the people by relaxing some of the pressures on them and offering important managerial and technical jobs to non-Communists. Bulgaria, Yugoslavia's other neighbor on the east, is having its troubles with production and is handicapped by a singularly uninspiring political leadership, but is still doing as well economically as comparable parts of Yugoslavia. Actually, the determining factors in the relative economic progress of the countries of Central and Southeastern Europe seem to be not the differences in economic systems but the differences, or similarities, in historical background, basic resources, and technical advancement. Titoism has not proved its superiority, at least not at this reading. The real contrast to Prague or Budapest is not Belgrade, but Vienna or Munich.

Yet two facts of prime importance dictate caution in pursuing that argument to its logical conclusion. The first is that Yugoslav society, with all its contradictions and disappointments, is *alive* — with ideas, with enterprise, with new forms of expression, with a search for practical truths in disregard of doctrinal "truth." The second is that Yugoslavia remains independent. It stands as an example, still a significant example despite the frustration of earlier hopes that its force of attraction would somehow draw other East

European states out of the Soviet bloc. It is ironic that the one satellite which seems successfully to have broken away from Moscow since 1948 is Yugoslavia's bitter enemy, Albania, whose leaders have found Soviet policy too revisionist, or Titoist, for their taste. Yet what has happened in Tirana illustrates the ferment and crosscurrents that exist within the bloc. As the ties which bind the satellites to Moscow are loosened, a trend which has been unmistakable despite the declarations of solidarity and the grandiose plans for economic integration, Yugoslavia cannot but exert an influence, not because of this or that set of institutions or reforms, but because of the simple fact of its independence.

The Future of Yugoslav Independence

The Yugoslavs face critical decisions on internal affairs: on the stimulation of economic growth and of exports, the expansion or contraction of recent reforms, the distribution of political power, the real meaning of industrial self-management, and the future role of the Communist Party. They face questions just as critical and as difficult to answer in determining the country's international position: how to judge the long-term prospects for neutralism, how strongly to cling to existing ties with the West, how far to move toward the East. Most important of all is the general direction of the regime's policies. Will the leaders preserve the "openings" to the free world — and to the Yugoslav people themselves — that have already been made?

The whole trend of Yugoslavia's development argues that they will, that they do not have an unlimited range of choice. It is true that the regime is essentially a dictatorship, and that dictatorships are capable of sudden turns of policy without accountability to anyone. It is also true that there are those among Yugoslavia's Communists who, whether or not they were "Cominformists" at one time or another, have never been happy about the increasing liberalization of the internal system or the running dispute with Moscow. Even with the top leaders themselves, brought up as they were in the world Communist movement, there is a certain feeling of "coming home" whenever they move toward better relations with Moscow. But these are rather shaky premises on which to spin a theory of impending fundamental change in Yugoslavia's position.

The more reliable signs of the times indicate that Tito does not intend such a change; that any subsequent or alternative leadership is likely to be guided by the same general considerations; and that the weight of popular will provides something close to a guarantee of the validity of those two propositions. The Yugoslav people have not all become converts to socialism, even in its comparatively mild Titoist form. For the most part they have accepted the system because there is no alternative and because a Yugoslav citizen, party member or not, can find a place for himself in it that is more than mere submission to his fate. Whether Yugoslav socialism is becoming more socialistic as time passes, or less so, is a matter for interpretation and argument, but there is little doubt that it becomes ever more Yugoslav.

If the Yugoslavs can be counted on in any event to safeguard their independence, to continue building their own system, and to keep useful ties with the West, we may wonder why we should be concerned at all. The difficulty lies in the fact that nothing can be counted on "in any event." If Yugoslavia's internal crisis deepens, if its economic position becomes much weaker, if the United States and other Western nations are totally unresponsive to Yugoslav needs, if the succession reveals unexpected stresses and conflicts, if the cold war enters an intensive phase with increasing Soviet pressures to bring Yugoslavia into line — if any or all of these things happen, no prediction can be sure.

Yugoslavia has a history marked by courageous struggles but hardly by continued stability under stress. Its nationality conflicts still rumble under the surface. Certainly it is not in the interest of the West, by what we do or fail to do, to encourage chaos, to aggravate Yugoslavia's problems, or to make its decisions more difficult than they are bound to be. The Yugoslavs, despite all the pressures to which they were subjected, came through the struggle with Stalin after 1948 thanks to their own determination and courage, but also because they had an anchor to the West.

That anchor has continued to be important to Tito's capacity to deal with the Soviet Union on his own terms. Ties with the neutralists are no substitute.

Yugoslavia may never provide what Charles McVicker has called a "pattern for international Communism." [1] But it does represent a society in which a Communist regime has undergone organic change, for both practical and human reasons. The new constitution appears to confirm that change. So long as its independence is maintained — and both government and people are firm in that resolve — Yugoslavia will have an influence inside and outside the Communist world that in the long run can only be of benefit to the West. Whatever the superficial appearances may be, as Yugoslavia makes its presence felt in Asia, Africa, and Latin America, it is not serving as the Kremlin's agent or torchbearer, although both are trying to combat the influence of China. Yugoslavia, as a small, independent socialist country, has its own purposes and its own appeal. Tito has won for himself and his country a considerable international prestige and freedom of action. He would not trade that for the status of a Kádár or even of a Gomulka. If his government talks about the sins of imperialism or the virtues of "peaceful coexistence," we have to interpret those words in the light of Yugoslavia's conduct and not in the fear that it is but the parroting of Soviet tactical slogans at Soviet behest.

Modest assistance, which is all Yugoslavia has been getting in recent years, is no great burden for the Western nations to carry. Surplus American wheat is of great help to Yugoslavia if it can be bought for Yugoslav dinars under Public Law 480 as in the past. To require payment in dollars, as the legislation extending Public Law 480 in October 1964 does, has the inevitable result of antagonizing Yugoslavia, worsening its international balance of payments, and reducing American influence. Even more important, the West should make adjustments to allow Yugoslavia to trade with the free world and to make its own way without discrimination. The restoration of most-favored-nation treatment to

[1] Charles P. McVicker, *Titoism: Pattern for International Communism* (New York: St. Martin's Press, 1957).

Yugoslavia by the United States in 1963 is a step in that direction. The Western nations will only be spiting themselves if they abandon a policy that has had real success and can have more, for it is based on a fundamental Yugoslav interest that is also in line with their own principles: that of national independence sustained by open and cooperative relations with other nations.

VI ALTERNATIVES
FOR AMERICAN POLICY

Uɴɪᴛᴇᴅ Sᴛᴀᴛᴇs objectives for Eastern Europe were set forth in the great documents of the wartime period: the Atlantic Charter, the United Nations Declaration, and the Yalta agreements. The nations liberated from Nazi Germany were to have their independence restored under governments of their own choosing. They were to have broadly representative provisional governments and then free elections. From the standpoint of the United States, this was a matter of principle. The nations of Eastern Europe had a right to self-determination, and the United States wished to see their independence restored to them. But was it also a matter of policy, which the United States would carry out even over the objection of one of its major allies in the war, the Soviet Union? It was obviously important to the West that Eastern Europe not be swept under Soviet domination. The destruction of German power, of course, would raise the question of where Soviet and Western power would meet in Europe and what kind of equilibrium would be established between them. At the time the Soviet armies swept into Eastern Europe, however, there was no real agreement with Stalin on that, nor was there any firm Western policy on whether and how to prevent Soviet domination.

Policy in the Immediate Postwar Period
The United States and Great Britain hoped that the general wartime statements of intent, which Stalin had also signed, would

be honored, and that he would not insist on establishing permanent Soviet hegemony. When he did so insist, by deed if not by word, they protested vigorously but they did not do anything effective to prevent it. This inaction has often been deplored, at the time and subsequently, by those who felt a stronger stand should have been taken. Let us merely take it as a fact based on Western conceptions of Western interests. The American government, and still less the British or the French, simply did not regard the establishment of Soviet domination, in the circumstances then prevailing, as so great a threat to Western security as to warrant a showdown with Moscow.

By February 1948 Soviet control, through Communist regimes loyal to Moscow, was complete — with the exception of Yugoslavia, which was forced out of the bloc later that same year because its leaders found that control unacceptable. These developments marked the end of the period of uncertainty. They sealed for some time the fate of the non-Communist parties and of the peoples of Eastern Europe. They were a defeat for the West. But, also, they highlighted the main issues on which the United States had to determine its objectives and its policies for the future: in particular, whether and how it would attempt to reverse what had happened.

The main objective, it was apparent from official pronouncements, was the same as was set forth in the statements of war aims: to secure for the peoples of Eastern Europe their right of self-determination. But the question of policy was now posed in somewhat different form. Whereas during the war the idea was to achieve that objective through defeating the Germans and cooperating with the Soviets, it had since been proved that the latter would not cooperate. Thus the objective, if it was to be attained at all, required a policy that would bring about the removal of Soviet domination now established and being rapidly consolidated. If the United States had not been willing to use force to prevent the imposition of Soviet rule on Eastern Europe when the situation there was in flux, and had not been able to prevent it by any other means, by what means could it end that rule and push the Soviets out? This was the dilemma that gave rise to the debate over containment and liberation which rocked America in the early 1950s.

"Containment" and "Liberation"

The policy of holding firm against Soviet expansion beyond the sphere of influence already established gradually took shape in 1946 and was given verbal form in President Truman's message to Congress on March 12, 1947. Its aim was support for the independence of free nations against pressures from outside and "armed minorities" from within. The immediate objects of support under the "Truman doctrine" were Greece and Turkey. With the adoption of the Marshall Plan it was apparent that Western Europe, where there were non-Communist governments or areas occupied by Western forces, was covered by American commitments. But what about countries further east? Where was the line to be drawn? Hungary, at the time of the "Truman doctrine" message, still had a coalition government led by a democrat, Ferenc Nagy, and based on the free election of 1945. In Czechoslovakia, President Beneš was trying to keep democracy afloat and to serve as a "bridge" between East and West. But Hungary was under Soviet occupation, and Czechoslovakia was following the Soviet line in foreign policy.

Sharp Soviet moves, to which the West made no effective response, settled the matter. A Communist coup brought the fall of the Nagy government in May 1947, a few days before Secretary of State George C. Marshall's Harvard speech, in which he stated the policies that were to become the Marshall Plan. Stalin vetoed Czechoslovakia's participation in the Marshall Plan, and in the following February the Communists took control in Prague. Thenceforward it was clear that in Europe containment began on the partition line in Germany (including the periphery of West Berlin), on the western borders of Czechoslovakia and Hungary, and on the frontiers of Greece and Turkey. In the Yugoslav sector the line moved, gradually and without clear statements of policy, from Trieste and the Adriatic to the borders of Hungary, Rumania, and Bulgaria. In their negotiations with the Soviet Union looking toward a settlement in Europe the Western powers directed their attention primarily to Austria and Germany where they had some bargaining power, rather than to Eastern Europe where they had none.

Did the Truman administration thereby write off the nations of Eastern Europe (except Yugoslavia)? It did not cease to state their right to freedom. It had as an ultimate objective the reduction and eventual elimination of dominant Soviet control over them. Yet it could not find policies, other than aid to heretic Yugoslavia, to bring about any progress in that direction. In the most authoritative statement of policy on the subject Marshall's successor as Secretary of State, Dean Acheson, taking account of the fact of Soviet domination, put the question squarely to the Soviet Union itself. If the Soviet leaders were interested in reducing tensions and in normal relations with the West, he said, let them withdraw their armed forces and police power from Eastern Europe and allow free elections.[1] Stalin was not that interested.

In the presidential campaign of 1952 the Republican leaders attacked existing American policy as negative and self-defeating, proposing to replace it with a policy of liberation of the peoples of Eastern Europe. In fairness to John Foster Dulles, the principal spokesman for the proposed new policy, it must be said that he never advocated the use of force to bring about liberation. In his most precise statement on the subject during the campaign he made the point that propaganda and intensified political warfare could bring the desired results without requiring the use of force. His argument was that American policy, if sufficiently dynamic, could make the enslavement of Eastern Europe so unprofitable that the Kremlin would let go its grip. By reviving and stimulating liberating influences American policies would set up strains and stresses in the Communist world which would make the Soviet rulers "impotent to continue in their monstrous ways and mark the beginning of their end."[2]

[1] Address at Berkeley, California, March 16, 1950 (see Appendix B).
[2] See John Foster Dulles, "A Policy of Boldness," *Life*, Vol. 32, No. 20,

Experience in office proved that America's power to liberate without unacceptable risks was less than had been promised. There was plenty of popular opposition to Soviet domination and to the local Communist regimes, more and more evident after the death of Stalin. But the East German uprising in 1953 showed that the decisive factor was the willingness of the Soviets to use force to maintain their position and the inability of the United States, avoiding the use of force, to change the situation.

Similarly the Hungarian revolt of 1956, which grew out of local conditions and owed little if anything to American policies, was suppressed by Soviet troops without America's doing anything to prevent it. Some have argued that the Western powers could have done something, but the fact is that they did not. In the crisis of 1956 Washington expressed the hope that the people of Poland and Hungary would make good their attempt to lessen the Soviet grip on their homelands and that the Soviet leadership would fulfill its pledges; as for the United States, it only wanted to see freedom restored to the captive nations and did not seek them as military allies.[3] These statements had no effect except perhaps to reassure the Kremlin that there would be no interference from the West.

Washington's decision was based on the conclusions that there was no way in which to exert effective influence at the time of crisis except by the use of force, that the Soviets were not bluffing, and that to use force would be to provoke a major war. Our Western European allies would not have supported the use of force, and it would not have been possible to obtain recommendations or decisions for it in the United Nations. Action in the United Nations was therefore limited to exhortation and condemnation.

The Concept of Gradualism

During President Eisenhower's second term little was said officially about liberation. The emphasis was on the gradual evolu-

May 19, 1952, pp. 146ff.; also Republican Party platform adopted July 10, 1952.

[3] Address of Secretary Dulles at Dallas, October 27, 1956 (see Appendix C); address of President Eisenhower, October 31, 1956.

tion of the captive states of Eastern Europe toward a status of greater independence of Soviet control. The United States, Secretary Dulles said, would do what it could to encourage that evolution. But the emphasis on political warfare, on setting up stresses and strains in the Soviet bloc so that the people could win their way to freedom, faded out. American propaganda, both through the official Voice of America and the unofficial Radio Free Europe, took on a much more moderate tone, avoiding themes that might stir up the peoples of Eastern Europe to hopeless revolt.

Economic aid to Poland was the best example of the new policy. It was intended to strengthen the new Polish regime, not against its people but in their interest, by giving it greater bargaining power in its relations with Moscow and flexibility in dealing with the West; the aid, most of it in the form of food, was intended also to help the Polish people and bring home to them America's interest in their welfare. Similarly, the United States continued its policy of aid to Yugoslavia, a policy dating from 1949, in spite of the off-again-on-again character of the Tito regime's relations with Moscow. So long as Yugoslavia was in fact independent in its domestic and foreign policies, as Washington concluded that it was, this aid served the purpose of strengthening that independence and of showing the governments of Eastern Europe that there was an alternative to total dependence on Moscow.

Leaving aside the exaggerated talk about dynamic policies and early liberation which prevailed in Washington during the mid-1950s, there has been in fact a continuity and a consistency about American policy toward Eastern Europe since the Soviet takeover. It has been based on (a) unwillingness to consider, or formally to accept, Soviet domination of the nations of Eastern Europe as just or as permanent; (b) efforts to build up the strength of the free world both for its own defense and for the general improvement of the West's position, so that any shifts or negotiated settlements affecting the overall balance in the cold war might have beneficial effects in Eastern Europe as elsewhere; and (c) recognition that changes in the *status quo* by a direct challenge or the use of force across the line of the curtain carry unacceptable risks — especially in the age of massive nuclear power on both sides, though the proposition held true even before the Soviet Union had such power.

The United States through a series of presidents and secretaries of state has not ceased, ever since the Second World War, to proclaim its hope that the captive nations will again have their freedom and its desire to see that end accomplished. The Congress, through the Captive Nations Resolution passed unanimously in 1959, has also proclaimed that it is vital to the national security of the United States that the desire for liberty and independence of the nations subjugated by the imperialistic policies of Communist Russia should be steadfastly kept alive; and that the United States shares with them their aspirations for recovery of that freedom and independence.[4] It is a little difficult to relate these statements to actual policy, but they do represent a generally held sentiment and a hoped-for outcome.

Actually, the Resolution's sweeping "whereas" clauses and emphasis on total liberation were not consistent with the steps currently being taken by the Eisenhower administration in its relations with the Eastern European regimes. American aid continued to go to Poland through the Polish government. Most-favored-nation treatment of Polish imports, cut off in 1951, was restored in 1960. The ban on American travel to Hungary was removed. Diplomatic relations with Bulgaria, suspended in 1950, were restored in 1960. The United States and Rumania instituted a cultural exchange program.

By 1960 the Eastern European question was no longer a sharp issue in American politics. Senator John F. Kennedy, during the course of his campaign for the presidency, offered a number of suggestions for getting in closer touch with nations with whom we had traditional ties, particularly Poland, in the hope of reduc-

---

[4] Public Law 86–90, 86th Congress, 1st Session, July 17, 1959. The Resolution is not confined to the satellite states of Eastern Europe, naming also the Baltic states, all the Communist states of Asia, and a number of units within the U.S.S.R. (e.g., Ukraine, "White Ruthenia," and "Cossackia"). See Appendix D.

ing their dependence on Moscow. He thought more flexible economic policies might contribute to that end. He emphasized the evolutionary character of his recommendations and deprecated rash promises to the captive peoples. His opponent, Vice-President Richard Nixon, in a last-minute proposal promised to go to Eastern Europe, if elected, to remind the world that those peoples would one day be delivered out of bondage, but that proposal never had to be tested; and Nixon, like Kennedy, disclaimed any purpose of trying to stir up revolts that were bound to fail.

The Kennedy and Johnson administrations have opened up no new frontiers in Eastern Europe. The spectacular events of recent years have been generated inside the Communist camp itself, not in Washington. The United States has continued the evolutionary and gradualist approach of the latter years of the Eisenhower administration. It has continued some aid to Poland. It renewed the cultural agreement with Rumania and encouraged expanded cultural contacts with Bulgaria. It has virtually dropped the "Hungarian case" at the United Nations, thus moving toward a normalization of relations with Hungary although certain obstacles (notably Cardinal Mindszenty's presence in the United States legation in Budapest) still remain. More notable than what we have done, perhaps, at a time when the Communist world has been rent by a great schism, when some Eastern European governments have been displaying an unexpected degree of independence and others an unexpected degree of confusion, is the fact that we have done so little to encourage those trends.

One reason is that American initiatives have no guarantee of favorable results in these disputes among Communists which are now benefiting the West anyway; indeed, such initiatives might be counterproductive in pushing the Communist states back into a greater solidarity against the West. In the case of the one satellite that has really broken free of Moscow in the last five years, Albania, there was little the West could do because Albania's declared loyalty was to Stalinism and its solidarity was with Peking. Another reason for comparative inaction has been the difficulty of dealing with the Eastern European regimes, especially since the clash of ideology with its war of words was still going on. A related factor is the lack of freedom and flexibility which makes it difficult for the executive branch of the government to develop policies which might take greater advantage of the situation.

It is ironic that, at the very time when the monolith is breaking up and the Soviet grip on Eastern Europe has been loosened, much of public and congressional opinion in the United States has veered sharply in the direction of an inflexible anti-Communism that makes no distinction among various types of Communist states, regardless of their respective power, size, policies, and degree of hostility to the West. Even Yugoslavia, a recipient of American aid for many years because of its independent stance, has often been put into the same category as the states of the bloc although it professes and practices neutralism (admittedly, Tito's comradely rapprochement with Khrushchev did not help his standing in this country). Privately organized boycotts have cut into the sales of Yugoslav and Polish goods. Most-favored-nation treatment was withdrawn from Poland and Yugoslavia by the Trade Expansion Act of 1962 and was just barely restored in the Foreign Assistance Act of 1963. Economic aid to any Communist country is virtually ruled out under current legislation.

Thus, an important question is posed. The development of policies which have elements of greater tolerance for regimes that are not only Communist but also still allies of the Soviet Union requires some soft-pedaling of ideological issues. To be successful, moreover, such policies often need a minimum rather than a maximum of publicity and public explanation. On the other hand, the executive branch must be responsive to public and congressional views.

If the executive is in fact hamstrung by limitations on its initiative and its flexibility of action in the changing situation in Eastern Europe, then perhaps a great debate is needed. Secretary of State Dean Rusk put his own views before the public recently in arguing for a flexible policy allowing differentiation in dealing with Communist states.[5] Some members of Congress have taken exception

[5] See Appendix E.

to his views. This matter might well be considered in connection with the ensuing discussion of alternative policies open to the United States.

Policies of Other Western States

While the United States has played a leading role in Western policy toward Eastern Europe, it cannot itself determine that policy. The major states of Western Europe also have their own ideas and their own interests. Because the degree of agreement and common action the West can attain has much to do with the effectiveness of any Western policy, a brief summary of the interests and attitudes of Great Britain, France, and the Federal Republic of Germany may be useful.

During the war the British were more directly concerned than the Americans over the shape of postwar Europe. Churchill did not view with equanimity the Soviet insistence on a "friendly" (i.e., Soviet-controlled) Poland and the prospect of Soviet domination of Hungary and the Balkans. Diplomacy, however, did not prove an adequate means of preventing what happened. Under the postwar Labour government Britain stood together with the United States in protesting Soviet treaty violations and the denial of self-determination, but it no longer attempted to have an active policy in Eastern Europe. There was no substantial change after the Conservatives returned to power in 1951. Great Britain and the United States have maintained a fairly solid front on the German question, although in their zeal to find a basis for negotiation with Moscow the British have shown a greater receptiveness to ideas such as disengagement and dealing with East Germany. Leaders of the Labour Party have leaned even more in that direction. There has been no support in Britain for a dynamic policy aimed at liberation of Eastern Europe, either in the Dulles period or since.

France, which played a leading role in Eastern Europe before World War II, was left out of the Yalta and Potsdam conferences and had no part in the postwar controversy over the denial of independence to the Eastern European nations, except to join a tripartite protest over the Communist coup in Czechoslovakia in 1948. It accepted the loss of its old political and economic positions but tried to save what it could of French cultural influence. At Bermuda in 1953 the French premier joined with President Eisenhower and Prime Minister Churchill to declare that the three powers did not regard the situation in Eastern Europe as just or as permanent. General de Gaulle has made that point more positively on his own. He has also stated, at a press conference on March 25, 1959, that France favors reunification of the two parts of Germany, provided the Germans do not reopen the question of their present frontiers, including the Oder-Neisse line. Although he has encouraged trade and cultural relations with Eastern Europe, he has developed no comprehensive policy and taken no initiative to negotiate on these matters with the Soviet leaders or anyone else. He has taken the position that at the present time it is fruitless to negotiate on Germany or on Central and Eastern Europe. But he aims eventually at a settlement ending the partition of the Continent and might not await American permission or agreement when he thought the time ripe to reach for it. He has spoken vaguely of the need to create a Europe "from the Atlantic to the Urals." What that idea means and where the nations of Eastern Europe fit into it is anybody's guess. Foreign Minister Couve de Murville has described it as a settlement made possible when equilibrium returns to Europe through the uniting of Western Europe and sufficient change and opening up of Russia; in other words, "a Europe balanced between East and West."[6]

The Federal Republic of Germany is the Western nation most directly concerned because East Germany is a part of the Soviet bloc and because of the problems of past and present that complicate Germany's relations with the Eastern European nations and with Russia itself. The primary objectives of Bonn's foreign policy have been the return of Germany to an equal and accepted position in the European community and the reunification of the country. Neither the Western powers nor the Federal Republic itself has been able to make any progress toward the latter objective, Soviet terms being unacceptable; and so the satellite status

[6] Interview on German television, June 28, 1963.

of East Germany has been indefinitely prolonged. Meanwhile, Bonn's relations with the Eastern European states have been limited by (a) the absence of diplomatic relations (because of their maintaining relations with East Germany), (b) Bonn's unwillingness to accept the Oder-Neisse line as the legal Polish-German frontier, and (c) the strong anti-German feeling in Poland and Czechoslovakia, which Moscow and the Polish and Czechoslovak regimes have tried to keep at a high pitch. The Federal Republic, somewhat more flexible in Eastern policy under Erhard than under Adenauer, has established trade missions in Poland, Hungary, Rumania, and Bulgaria, and has built up its trade with Eastern Europe. These trade relations have, of course, served German commercial interests, but they have also contributed to the general process of increasing contacts between Eastern Europe and the West.

Alternatives for Present and Future: Objectives

Official policies, as the record shows, have been neither wholly consistent nor beyond criticism. Indeed, Eastern Europe is one field where opinions within America and within the Western community have often differed. Now that the Communist world is undergoing its own crisis, with increasing challenges to the leading role of the Soviet Union, it is an opportune time to re-examine both the assumptions and the directions of American policy. The exposition of objectives and alternative policies which follows is presented as background for discussion. It is not intended as argument for any particular line or to be loaded on one side or another.

The following points appear to be generally accepted objectives of the United States in Eastern Europe. Are they still valid? Are they mutually consistent? What are the priorities? Some pertinent questions appear following each point.

1. The reduction and eventual elimination of the Soviet military presence in Eastern Europe.

a. Are these troops and facilities (some twenty divisions in

East Germany and about six altogether in Poland and Hungary) a significant threat to Western Europe?

b. Would their withdrawal to the U.S.S.R. (with no comparable Western withdrawal) give the West an important strategic advantage?

c. What price, in terms of a Western withdrawal, would be worth paying for that advantage?

d. What political advantages do they give the Soviets?

e. Would their departure enable Eastern Europe to free itself from Soviet dominance or from Communist rule?

f. Could they not return at Moscow's will?

2. Achievement of greater independence for the Eastern European states, eventually to the point where their foreign policies are not determined by any outside power (as they are now by the U.S.S.R. or, in the case of Albania, by Communist China) and they are free to determine their own relations with the Soviet Union and with the Western nations.

a. Can the United States reach this goal by support of national Communism or only by working for the disappearance of Communism from Eastern Europe?

b. Could Finland, Austria, or Yugoslavia be considered models for those states now in the Warsaw Pact?

c. Should Western policies toward Yugoslavia be aimed toward affecting the course taken by the satellites?

d. Can the United States propose neutrality for Eastern Europe while not accepting it for Germany?

e. Should Western European organizations envisage the ultimate inclusion of Eastern European states?

3. Unification of Germany through free elections in both the Federal Republic and the Soviet zone.

a. Is German unification a necessary first step in the process of gaining greater freedom and independence for the nations of Eastern Europe?

b. Should the German and Eastern European questions be combined in package proposals (e.g., the Rapacki Plan or some variant of it) or kept separate?

    c. Should the United States rigidly exclude East Germany from policies aimed at increasing contacts with Eastern European regimes and peoples?

4. Free choice by the Eastern European peoples of their own governments and political institutions.

    a. Is this really an objective of American policy or merely a development we should eventually like to see take place?

    b. Is it consistent with the encouragement of greater national independence of the existing regimes (the second objective mentioned above)?

    c. To what extent is the United States committed to this objective, through international agreements, official declarations, the Captive Nations Resolution, moral obligations, or the principles of its own system?

The above objectives do not include victory over Communism and its destruction both in Eastern Europe and in the Soviet Union itself. There is a real question whether such an objective could be reached in any other way than by war, if it is attainable at all. It is only fair to say that those who advocate it do not all propose launching a war; many believe that the desired end may be attained if the United States will undertake a political offensive involving some risks of war, on the grounds that the Soviets fear war more than we and will back down as they did in Cuba in 1962. Such a strategy, which received some attention in the presidential campaign of 1964, is worthy of discussion on its own merits, as it is pertinent to the gaining of other objectives less far-reaching than the end of Communism.

At the other end of the spectrum is the objective of achieving understanding and agreement with the Soviet Union as a primary end in itself, even to the point of formally accepting the continued division of Germany and the *status quo* in Eastern Europe in the interest of ending the cold war and preventing a hot one. Such an objective may be dismissed by many as appeasement. However, since some points of view in this country and in Europe come close to it, it should be kept in mind as part of the background for the consideration of policies open to the United States.

Alternatives for Present and Future: Policies

Alternative courses for the United States are brought together here under three general lines of policy. It is not maintained that they include all possible actions, or that they are mutually exclusive. The first and third fit into different strategies for dealing with the Soviet Union, what might be called the hard line and the soft line. The second is directed more particularly to Eastern Europe, without so strong a commitment one way or the other on overall strategy toward the Soviet Union.

1. One clear line of policy is the stepping up of political and economic warfare against Soviet and Communist rule in Eastern Europe. It assumes continuation of the cold war and would attempt to capitalize on the present troubles and uncertainty within the bloc, disrupt the plans and policies of the Communist regimes, and strengthen popular resistance to them. It would regard the bloc as a whole, assuming an identity of interest between Moscow and the satellite regimes, with the latter the weakest points and most suitable targets of political warfare. This is essentially a continuation of the declared Dulles policy of liberation, based on the idea that pressure on the Eastern European states from outside, the creation of political and economic strains, and the support of the idea of freedom can generate changes in the direction of freedom. But it involves pushing harder than the United States did in the Dulles period. The aim would be to overthrow the satellite regimes and free the captive peoples from the Soviet empire, singly or as a group, as opportunities develop. Such political defeats would shake the whole structure of the Communist world, including the U.S.S.R. itself. This policy does not envisage encouraging open revolt that would only be crushed by the Soviets, but it involves taking some risks of armed conflict and does not shirk a confrontation with the Soviet Union should a revolutionary situation develop in one or more of the satellite states.

Such a policy might have the following specific aspects:

a. *In diplomacy.* The United States would keep raising the issue of freedom for Eastern Europe, in direct negotiations with the Soviet Union and at the United Nations. It would propose immediate free elections in Eastern Europe as well as in Germany. It would proceed on the theory that a time of comparative Soviet weakness over economic troubles and the split with China is a time to press for Soviet concessions. It would demand political concessions such as changes in the internal policies of the satellite regimes in return for trade and aid, in contrast to our handling of wheat sales to the Soviet Union and Hungary and to the policy of giving aid to Yugoslavia and Poland without political conditions.

b. *In propaganda.* American propaganda would attack the Communist rulers on a broad front, stressing their denial of freedom to the people and (in the case of satellite leaders) their role as Soviet puppets. It would expose the falsity of their use of nationalist slogans and of their allegedly nationalist and independent policies. It would turn the "colonialism" issue against Soviet colonialism in Eastern Europe. Supplemented by covert operations, it would encourage and help to organize popular resistance to Communist rule, using the cooperation of exiles in building an alternative leadership.

c. *In military policy.* Since a position of military strength is essential to a strong and forceful waging of political warfare as well as for deterrence and defense, the United States would maintain the strongest possible military position in Europe and urge all NATO members to do the same. It would not risk weakening that position by experiments in disengagement, atom-free zones, or arms control. It would seek to exploit the basic weakness which unreliable satellite armies and hostile populations in Eastern Europe represent for the Soviet Union and the satellite regimes.

d. *In trade and aid.* The United States, and, it would hope, its allies, would use economic instruments to the fullest possible extent as a means of weakening the Communist bloc, especially in Eastern Europe. It would provide no aid to Communist governments. It would rigidly control trade, so that Western goods could not be used to strengthen the military potential of the bloc or to help the Communist regimes succeed in their economic plans. Trade would be used as a political weapon; shipments of urgently needed food or other goods would be used to win political concessions. The mere fact of trade relations would not be considered as promoting independence or helping the people because of the total political control exercised by the pro-Soviet Communist regimes.

e. *In cultural relations.* It would be assumed that nothing would be gained by developing cultural exchanges, since the Communist regimes use them for their own political purposes (e.g., to gather intelligence) and their own prestige, and can control them closely and reduce or eliminate them if they find them a net disadvantage. As national cultures have been stifled by the Communist regimes in Eastern Europe, support would be given to the efforts of exiles in the free world to maintain and develop their traditional cultures.

2. The second line of policy, recognizing the interrelationship between the Soviet Union and the countries of Eastern Europe, nonetheless distinguishes between them and aims to weaken the ties that bind them together. It assumes a condition of something less than total dependence of the Eastern European regimes on Moscow and the possibility that the gulf may be widened to the breaking point, as happened with Yugoslavia in 1948. It assumes also the possibility of changes in the nature of those regimes and in the degree of common interest they have with their own peoples. The United States, accordingly, would maintain normal relations with the Eastern European states. It would encourage their national interests rather than the sectarian interests of their regimes, though admittedly on some issues the difference might be irrelevant or impossible to ascertain. It would offer them alternatives to exclusive reliance on Moscow, along lines that would be supported by their peoples. The policy would take form through a multiplicity of contacts and influences. In essence, it would try to rebuild the historic ties between the West and the Eastern European states, though not necessarily a military or an organic political connection. The Eastern European states might move

toward a status like that of Yugoslavia, or possibly Finland or Austria. This would be a gradual process, taking place by a succession of small steps rather than by a major showdown with the Soviet Union.

Such a policy might have the following specific aspects:

  a. *In diplomacy.* The United States would deal with the Eastern European regimes as with other governments, although without formally giving up the basic position that Communist rule had been established by Soviet power in violation of treaty obligations. It would examine all proposals of disengagement, regional arms control, mutual reduction of forces, etc. — and perhaps make some of its own — from the standpoint of their potential effects in increasing the freedom of maneuver and bargaining power of the Eastern European states with the Soviet Union, giving this factor full weight alongside the military considerations and risks. In Poland and Czechoslovakia, Western policy would aim at diminishing the fear of Germany, perhaps through pledges and guarantees (including recognition of the Oder-Neisse line) and by encouraging the German Federal Republic to reach mutually satisfactory agreements with Eastern European states, especially with Poland. In pursuing the aim of German unification, the Western powers, including the German Federal Republic, would take full account of Polish and Czechoslovak concern for security and territorial integrity. The West would seek opportunities to associate the Eastern European states with the work of the United Nations and other international organizations where they might see their own national interests as different from those of the Soviet Union. Western diplomacy would be prepared to act swiftly in support of any state moving toward or into a situation similar to Yugoslavia's in 1948. It would encourage, in negotiations with the Soviets and otherwise, the idea of neutrality for Eastern Europe.

  b. *In propaganda.* American propaganda would not stop telling the truth about Communism or contesting the falsehoods put out by the Communist regimes, but the emphasis would be on the issue of independence versus dependence. All available means of communication would be used to increase intellectual contacts with both regimes and peoples, stressing national interests as opposed to Soviet interests and ideological lines set by Moscow. Full publicity on the Soviet-Chinese conflict and on the factional struggles among Communists all over the world should help to weaken ideology as a cement holding the bloc together. Covert propaganda might be used to encourage further loosening of the internal situation in the Eastern European countries, so long as it was handled carefully and did not negate the main purpose of the policy.

c. *In military policy.* Maintenance of a position of strength in Western Europe would continue to be necessary. If the West is to exert influence on Eastern Europe, it must be able to prevent Soviet threats and military adventures on the western side of the iron curtain. However, in order to encourage Eastern European governments to consider new steps toward independence, or to encourage Moscow to consider negotiating some changes in current military positions, the United States would be prepared to explore the possibilities of changes in Western dispositions and reciprocal reduction or withdrawal of forces or other comparable measures. Because withdrawal of Soviet forces from Hungary, Poland, and East Germany would create an atmosphere favorable to greater political independence on the part of Eastern European states, the whole question of military dispositions would be included in a careful study of what price might safely be paid to obtain that result.

d. *In trade and aid.* The United States would attempt to expand its trade with Eastern Europe, putting it on a basis different from trade with the Soviet Union, in order to build up economic ties and interests which would make Eastern European states less dependent on Moscow and would keep them looking westward. It would also differentiate among Eastern European states. Above all, Western Europe's trade with Eastern Europe (which is far greater than ours) would be encouraged. The resulting multiplicity of economic contacts and the quality of Western goods would open the doors to greater Western influence. The political benefits of expanding economic relations would be regarded as outweighing the possible danger to Western security from the increment in the bloc's military or economic potential. Extension of economic or technical assistance to Eastern European states would be regarded in the same light. Aid would be continued to Poland as long as it served that purpose. It would be continued to Yugoslavia as a support to that country's independence and an example to others in Eastern Europe. Inclusion of others in the American aid program would await further evolution in their position and policies.

e. *In cultural relations.* Following the same argument of the more contacts with Eastern Europe the better, the United States would pursue educational and other exchanges with the idea of punching holes in the iron curtain, establishing contacts with the peoples of Eastern Europe, and exerting some influence on the governments.

3. The third line of policy is directed to the U.S.S.R. as well as Eastern Europe, in fact, primarily to the U.S.S.R. It would not make a point of trying to split the satellites off from the Soviet bloc, on the ground that this would make the essential policy of détente with Moscow more difficult and probably is impossible anyway. It is based on the assumption that things are changing in the Soviet Union as well as in the satellites; what the United States should seek, therefore, is a general liberalization affecting all Communist society (leaving aside China), not just the relations between Communist states. Under this approach, there would be no distinctions made in Western trade and cultural relations between the Eastern European states and the Soviet Union. As all are relatively satisfied societies (compared to China) and want time to work out their own economic problems and give greater satisfaction to their own peoples, this view holds, they will tend to lose their revolutionary drive and to look toward greater cooperation with the West. Thus it is assumed that for the Soviets

peaceful coexistence is more than a propaganda slogan, or at least that the trend is in that direction. This trend is helped along by the split with China, which the Soviet Union will regard increasingly not only as a rival in the world Communist movement but as a threat to its own security. It will be inclined to trade more with the West, allowing the satellites to do the same, and eventually to see the sharp edges of the cold war dulled by a basic common interest in peace. An American policy emphasizing coexistence rather than cold war, without being taken in by Soviet deception or conceding essential interests, could pave the way in due course for closer relations with the whole Soviet bloc, for eventual major settlements in Europe that would offer security to the West, and for the disappearance of the most dangerous features of the cold war. Only with a general relaxation of the cold war would the Eastern European states be allowed by the Kremlin to enjoy any real independence.

Such a policy might have the following specific aspects:

a. *In diplomacy.* American diplomacy would endeavor to keep all outstanding unsettled questions under negotiation with Moscow. It would build on the common desire to avoid risks of nuclear war. It would seek agreements in Europe that would reduce tensions and improve the atmosphere for further agreements. This would not mean recognizing Soviet dominance in Eastern Europe or the permanent partition of Germany, but it could mean keeping these questions on the shelf while concentrating on such matters as limited disarmament in Central Europe, disengagement, and greater freedom of trade. Concessions would not be made to the Soviets merely to reduce tensions or in the hope that the force of example and an atmosphere of trust would encourage Soviet concessions, but the door would be kept open to all possible agreements based on mutual advantage.

b. *In propaganda.* American propaganda to the Soviet Union and Eastern Europe would be kept at a low pitch, emphasizing the theme of coexistence and the benefits of normal relations with the West. Common interests in peace and economic progress would be stressed and ideological warfare soft-pedaled. Channels of communication would be used to encourage a reasoned dialogue on matters separating East and West.

c. *In military policy.* The major concern would be to reduce the pressures and dangers of the East-West confrontation in Central Europe. The West would not unilaterally dismantle its military position, but it would abandon the idea of military strength as a means of forcing political concessions from the Soviets, actively seeking mutually acceptable military arrangements that might make political settlements likelier.

d. *In trade and aid.* The United States would abandon controls over exports to the Soviet Union and Eastern Europe (except on arms) on the ground that they have been no more than a minor irritant to the Soviets in the development of their economy but a major irritant in Soviet-American relations and within the Western alliance. Government guarantees of commercial credit would be used as a means of encouraging American exports to the U.S.S.R. and Eastern Europe. Trade between Western Europe and the Soviet Union and Eastern Europe (including arrangements between the Common Market and the Council for Mutual Economic Assistance) would be encouraged, in order to prevent the consolidation of separate economic blocs almost certain to generate economic warfare and mutual political hostility.

e. *In cultural relations.* For the same reasons, the United States and the West would promote and extend cultural and educational exchanges, official and unofficial, on the assumption that such contacts would favor the open over the relatively closed society. They could affect the thinking of the intelligentsia in Communist countries and of those who might have a role in future political leadership even though the structure of Communist Party rule remains more or less intact. They would tend to promote understanding between peoples and thus indirectly bring about better relations between governments.

General Considerations

Certain broad considerations should be kept in mind in the examination of these or any other American policies for Eastern Europe. Briefly, they have to do with the factors of space and time which relate any one problem to the whole context of foreign policy and to the trends of contemporary world politics.

As we have seen, from the Second World War to the present the fate of Eastern Europe has been a segment of the whole pattern of relations between the Soviet Union and the West and of the balance of power in the world. It is affected by what happens in Western Europe, the Middle East, Southeast Asia, China, or Japan, by changes in weapons and shifts in relative military or economic strength, or by negotiations over arms control or outer space. This is not an argument that nothing should be done about Eastern Europe until other problems are solved, merely a reminder that to overemphasize that one problem as *the* vital question of foreign policy (as has been done on occasion) is to narrow and distort our vision.

One fact in the broad picture of international relations that has put all others into a new perspective is the existence of nuclear weapons. It has become a cliché that the fate of the world now hangs on a balance of terror. All that need be said here is that the place where that balance is most delicate is Central and Eastern Europe. There, where the line of division between the Soviet and Western worlds is more rigid and probably more brittle than anywhere else, resort to force by a major power to change the status of a country or area from one bloc to the other is virtually ruled out because both are committed to meet force with force and the risks of a nuclear war of annihilation would be very high. The Soviet Union could use armed force against the unfortunate Hungarians in 1956, but it has not used armed force against West Berlin.

So far as the great powers are concerned, this situation has brought a fundamental change in the character of the competition for control of territory that has been for centuries the very substance of international relations. The nuclear balance has not, however, ruled out changes taking place other than by a direct East-West confrontation and showdown, as the case of Yugoslavia shows. Without reducing the importance of armed strength as an adjunct of successful diplomacy — a vital reason for keeping allied forces in West Germany and West Berlin — it gives added emphasis to political factors as the main determinants of the future.

The destiny of Eastern Europe and the course of the cold war will depend not only on what policies the Soviet Union and the Western powers may adopt now and in the next year or two but on developments we cannot possibly predict. Much hangs on what happens within Soviet society itself. Internal changes in the Soviet Union, whatever direction they take, are likely to find their reflection in Soviet attitudes toward the rest of the world. Who can say whether the Communist regime's relations with its own people will modify its ingrained antagonism toward the Western world? On the wider stage of relations among Communist states, who can say whether changing relations with China may make Soviet differences with the West over Eastern Europe a matter of fairly easy accommodation? The United States obviously cannot base policy on the assumption that these things are happening or soon will happen. But it is important that such trends not be foreclosed by policies that look no farther ahead than the immediate present.

Another area where decisive changes affecting Eastern Europe may take place is Western Europe. Will it grow in strength and unity or again fall victim to the clash of contending nationalisms? If the former, will it remain a partner of the United States or move toward the status of an independent third force between America and Russia? Will it, perhaps, find its own policies on Eastern Europe or its own accommodation with the Soviet Union regardless of American policies? The greatest question mark and in some ways the greatest danger is Germany because the German nation, a potential force for good or for evil, is itself split by the line of partition which runs through Europe. German nationalism could, in some not unforeseeable circumstances, help toward a stable settlement in Europe; in others, it could blow up the present uneasy peace or bring about a Soviet-German deal that would destroy the security of Western Europe and imperil the United States.

It is to be hoped that the unity in freedom which Western Europe attains will attract and in time absorb the Eastern European countries. A reduction of the dominant Soviet presence in the latter would contribute to that end, and in this process American policy may play its part. In any event, the United States should never forget the vital place which a secure and friendly Western Europe holds in its global policy. That is the top priority, which American policies for both parts of Europe should take into account.

A final point, one often made by the practitioners of foreign policy, is that its limitations must be borne in mind. What the United States can do directly to influence developments in the countries of Eastern Europe or to bring about changes in their relations with the Soviet Union or with the West is limited by the fact that Soviet power is very much present in that area. It is limited also by the fact that relations within the Communist world have their own dynamics; it was not Western policy that brought about the Tito-Stalin break or the revolt in Hungary. Western European interests, moreover, are closer and more immediately concerned than America's; our Western European allies cannot be counted on automatically to follow American policies in Eastern Europe which do not take account of their interests as they see them. This is hardly a positive note on which to conclude. There will be much that the United States can do. But successful policy is not made in a vacuum, in ignorance or in defiance of the actual conditions that prevail.

APPENDIXES

A YALTA DECLARATION ON LIBERATED EUROPE (February 11, 1945)

The Premier of the Union of Soviet Socialist Republics, the Prime Minister of the United Kingdom, and the President of the United States of America have consulted with each other in the common interests of the peoples of their countries and those of liberated Europe. They jointly declare their mutual agreement to concert during the temporary period of instability in liberated Europe the policies of their three Governments in assisting the peoples liberated from the domination of Nazi Germany and the peoples of the former Axis satellite states of Europe to solve by democratic means their pressing political and economic problems.

The establishment of order in Europe and the rebuilding of national economic life must be achieved by processes which will enable the liberated peoples to destroy the last vestiges of nazi-ism and fascism and to create democratic institutions of their own choice. This is a principle of the Atlantic Charter — the right of all peoples to choose the form of government under which they will live — the restoration of sovereign rights and self-government to those peoples who have been forcibly deprived of them by the aggressor nations.

To foster the conditions in which the liberated peoples may exercise these rights, the three Governments will jointly assist the people in any European liberated state or former Axis satellite state in Europe where in their judgment conditions require (a) to establish conditions of internal peace; (b) to carry out emergency measures for the relief of distressed peoples; (c) to form interim governmental authorities broadly representative of all democratic elements in the population and pledged to the earliest possible establishment through free elections of governments responsive to the will of the people; and (d) to facilitate where necessary the holding of such elections.

The three Governments will consult the other United Nations

SOURCE: *A Decade of American Foreign Policy, Basic Documents, 1941–49*; 81st Congress, 1st Session; Senate Document No. 123 (Washington, D.C.: Government Printing Office, 1950), p. 29.

and provisional authorities or other governments in Europe when matters of direct interest to them are under consideration.

When, in the opinion of the three Governments, conditions in any European liberated state or any former Axis satellite state in Europe make such action necessary, they will immediately consult together on the measures necessary to discharge the joint responsibilities set forth in this declaration.

By this declaration we reaffirm our faith in the principles of the Atlantic Charter, our pledge in the declaration by the United Nations, and our determination to build in cooperation with other peace-loving nations world order under law, dedicated to peace, security, freedom, and general well-being of all mankind.

In issuing this declaration, the three powers express the hope that the Provisional Government of the French Republic may be associated with them in the procedure suggested.

B EXCERPT FROM SPEECH BY DEAN
ACHESON, *Berkeley, California, March 16, 1950*

"TENSIONS BETWEEN THE UNITED STATES AND THE SOVIET UNION"

With regard to the whole group of countries which we are accustomed to think of as the satellite area, the Soviet leaders could withdraw their military and police force and refrain from using the shadow of that force to keep in power persons or regimes which do not command the confidence of the respective peoples, freely expressed through orderly representative processes. In other words, they could elect to observe, in practice, the declaration to which they set their signatures at Yalta concerning liberated Europe.

In this connection, we do not insist that these governments have any particular political or social complexion. What concerns us is that they should be truly independent national regimes, with a will of their own and with a decent foundation in popular feeling. We would like to feel, when we deal with these governments, that we are dealing with something representative of the national identity of the peoples in question. We cannot believe that such a situation would be really incompatible with the security of the Soviet Union.

This is a question of elementary good faith, and it is vital to a spirit of confidence that other treaties and other agreements will be honored. Nothing would so alter the international climate as the holding of elections in the satellite states in which the true will of the people could be expressed.

SOURCE: *Department of State Bulletin*, Vol. XXII, No. 560, March 27, 1950, pp. 475–476.

C EXCERPT FROM SPEECH BY JOHN FOSTER DULLES, Dallas, Texas, October 27, 1956

"THE TASK OF WAGING PEACE"

Another intensive concern of our foreign policy is in relation to the captive nations of the world. We had looked upon World War II as a war of liberation. The Atlantic Charter and the United Nations Declaration committed all the Allies to restore sovereign rights and self-government to those who had been forcibly deprived of them and to recognize the right of all peoples to choose the form of government under which they would live. Unhappily, those pledges have been violated, and in Eastern Europe one form of conquest was merely replaced by another.

But the spirit of patriotism, and the longing of individuals for freedom of thought and of conscience and the right to mold their own lives, are forces which erode and finally break the iron bonds of servitude.

Today we see dramatic evidence of this truth. The Polish people now loosen the Soviet grip upon the land they love. And the heroic people of Hungary challenge the murderous fire of Red Army tanks. These patriots value liberty more than life itself. And all who peacefully enjoy liberty have a solemn duty to seek, by all truly helpful means, that those who now die for freedom will not have died in vain. It is in this spirit that the United States and others have today acted to bring the situation in Hungary to the United Nations Security Council.

The weakness of Soviet imperialism is being made manifest. Its weakness is not military weakness nor lack of material power. It is weak because it seeks to sustain an unnatural tyranny by suppressing human aspirations which cannot indefinitely be suppressed and by concealing truths which cannot indefinitely be hidden.

Imperialist dictatorships often present a formidable exterior. For a time they may seem to be hard, glittering, and irresistible. But

SOURCE: *Documents on American Foreign Relations, 1956* (New York: Harper and Brothers, 1957), pp. 44–46.

in reality they turn out to be "like unto whited sepulchres, which indeed appear beautiful outward, but are within full of dead men's bones, and of all uncleanness." They have vulnerabilities not easily seen.

Our Nation has from its beginning stimulated political independence and human liberty throughout the world. Lincoln said of our Declaration of Independence that it gave "liberty not alone to the people of this country, but hope to all the world, for all future time." During the period when our Nation was founded, the tides of despotism were running high. But our free society and its good fruits became known throughout the world and helped to inspire the subject peoples of that day to demand, and to get, the opportunity to mold their own destinies.

Today our Nation continues its historic role. The captive peoples should never have reason to doubt that they have in us a sincere and dedicated friend who shares their aspirations. They must know that they can draw upon our abundance to tide themselves over the period of economic adjustment which is inevitable as they rededicate their productive efforts to the service of their own people, rather than of exploiting masters. Nor do we condition economic ties between us upon the adoption by these countries of any particular form of society.

And let me make this clear, beyond a possibility of doubt: The United States has no ulterior purpose in desiring the independence of the satellite countries. Our unadulterated wish is that these peoples, from whom so much of our own national life derives, should have sovereignty restored to them and that they should have governments of their own free choosing. We do not look upon these nations as potential military allies. We see them as friends and as part of a new and friendly and no longer divided Europe. We are confident that their independence, if promptly accorded, will contribute immensely to stabilize peace throughout all of Europe, West and East.

D *THE CAPTIVE NATIONS RESOLUTION*
(July 1959)

Joint (Senate) Resolution, Adopted by the Senate
July 6, 1959 and the House July 8, 1959

WHEREAS the greatness of the United States is in large part attributable to its having been able, through the democratic process, to achieve a harmonious national unity of its people, even though they stem from the most diverse of racial, religious, and ethnic backgrounds; and

WHEREAS this harmonious unification of the diverse elements of our free society has led the people of the United States to possess a warm understanding and sympathy for the aspirations of peoples everywhere and to recognize the natural interdependency of the peoples and nations of the world; and

WHEREAS the enslavement of a substantial part of the world's population by Communist imperialism makes a mockery of the idea of peaceful coexistence between nations and constitutes a detriment to the natural bonds of understanding between the people of the United States and other peoples; and

WHEREAS since 1918 the imperialistic and aggressive policies of Russian communism have resulted in the creation of a vast empire which poses a dire threat to the security of the United States and of all the free peoples of the world; and

WHEREAS the imperialistic policies of Communist Russia have led, through direct and indirect aggression, to the subjugation of the national independence of Poland, Hungary, Lithuania, Ukraine, Czechoslovakia, Latvia, Estonia, White Ruthenia, Rumania, East Germany, Bulgaria, mainland China, Armenia, Azerbaijan, Georgia, North Korea, Albania, Idel-Ural, Tibet, Cossackia, Turkestan, North Viet-Nam, and others; and

WHEREAS these submerged nations look to the United States, as the citadel of human freedom, for leadership in bringing about their liberation and independence and in restoring to them the

SOURCE: Public Law 86–90, 86th Congress, 1st Session, July 17, 1959.

enjoyment of their Christian, Jewish, Moslem, Buddhist, or other religious freedoms, and of their individual liberties; and

WHEREAS it is vital to the national security of the United States that the desire for liberty and independence on the part of the peoples of these conquered nations should be steadfastly kept alive; and

WHEREAS the desire for liberty and independence by the overwhelming majority of the people of these submerged nations constitutes a powerful deterrent to war and one of the best hopes for a just and lasting peace; and

WHEREAS it is fitting that we clearly manifest to such peoples through an appropriate and official means the historic fact that the people of the United States share with them their aspirations for the recovery of their freedom and independence: Now, therefore, be it

Resolved by the Senate and House of Representatives of the United States of America in Congress assembled, That the President of the United States is authorized and requested to issue a proclamation designating the third week in July 1959 as "Captive Nations Week" and inviting the people of the United States to observe such week with appropriate ceremonies and activities. The President is further authorized and requested to issue a similar proclamation each year until such time as freedom and independence shall have been achieved for all the captive nations of the world.

E   *EXCERPT FROM SPEECH BY DEAN RUSK,*
Washington, D.C., February 25, 1964

"WHY WE TREAT DIFFERENT COMMUNIST COUNTRIES
DIFFERENTLY"

Until the Communists themselves change, the most elementary
security considerations demand that we remain ever alert to the
dangers their very outlook on life raises for us and for others committed to freedom.

But our policy does not end there. In the longer run, we want the
Communists to come to see that their aggressive hostility toward
the Free World is not only costly and dangerous but futile. Meanwhile, we want to reduce as much as we can the chance that the
hostility they have created between them and us may lead to a
great war. Thus we search patiently for agreements and understandings to settle or blunt dangerous disputes between us and to
bring armaments under control. The Soviets appear to recognize
that there is a common interest in preventing a mutually destruc-
tive thermonuclear exchange. We have managed to reach a few
limited agreements with them. These do not yet constitute a *détente*. We hope for further agreements or understandings. But in
the field of disarmament there are severe limits to the progress that
can be made without reliable inspection and verification of arms
retained. And on many vital political issues, Moscow's views and
the West's remain far apart. Nevertheless, we shall pursue un-
ceasingly our earnest quest for mutually acceptable steps toward
a more reliable peace.

But it is not enough to "contain" communism and to try to negotiate specific agreements to reduce the danger of a great war.
The conflict between the Communists and the Free World is as
fundamental as any conflict can be. Their proclaimed objectives
and our conception of a decent world order just do not and cannot
fit together.

We view communism as a system incapable of satisfying basic

SOURCE: *Department of State Bulletin,* Vol. L, No. 1290, March 16, 1964,
pp. 390–396.

human needs, as a system which will ultimately be totally discredited in the minds of men everywhere. We believe that the peoples who have been brought under Communist rule aspire to a better life — of peace, economic opportunity, and a chance to pursue happiness. This, indeed, has always been so. But in recent years an important new trend has been perceptible: some of the Communist governments have become responsive, in varying degrees, if not directly to the aspirations of their subjects, at least to kindred aspirations of their own. The Communist world is no longer a single flock of sheep following blindly behind one leader.

The Soviet Union and Communist China are engaged in a deep and comprehensive quarrel — involving ideology (how best to promote the Communist world revolution), a struggle for influence in other countries and other Communist parties, conflicting national interests, and personal rivalries. The dispute between Moscow and Peiping has spread through the world Communist movement and, in many countries, has divided the local parties.

The Chinese Communists have demanded that the Russians risk their national interests, and even their national survival, to promote the world revolution, as that cause is defined by Peiping. The rulers of the Soviet Union have rejected this doctrine. They appear to have begun to realize that there is an irresolvable contradiction between the demands to promote world communism by force and the needs and interests of the Soviet state and people.

The smaller Communist countries of Eastern Europe have increasingly, although in varying degree, asserted their own policies. We have always considered it unnatural for the diverse peoples of Eastern Europe, with their own talents and proud traditions, to be submerged in a monolithic bloc. We have wanted these peoples, while living in friendship with their Russian and other neighbors, to develop in accordance with their own national aspirations and genius. And they seem to feel a strong nostalgia for their traditional ties with the West. Most of them are increasing their trade and other contacts with Western Europe and, to some extent, with us.

Within the Soviet bloc, the Stalinist terror has been radically changed. And within the Soviet Union as well as most of the smaller European Communist nations there are signs — small but varied and persistent signs — of yearnings for more individual freedom. And there are practical reasons why men must be allowed freedom — if they are to achieve their best.

Throughout the Communist world, the economic shortcomings of communism are vividly manifest. Failures in food production have become endemic. In Communist China, the standard of living is even lower than it was before the calamitous collapse of the "Great Leap Forward." The Soviet rate of growth has dropped below that of the United States and Western Europe and far below that of Japan. The actual increase in income, both national and per capita, in the last twelve years was less in the Soviet Union than in the United States. The fact that communism is economically inefficient has become increasingly plain to most of the peoples of the world.

Here let us note a few points about trade. Since 1948 we have used export controls to keep strategic commodities from the Soviet Union and its European satellites. Since 1950 we have maintained a total embargo on trade with Communist China and North Korea; and somewhat later this embargo was extended to North Viet Nam. In October 1960, we embargoed exports to Cuba, excepting foods and medicines. All these actions were taken and have been maintained for what seem to us to be very good reasons. In controlling exports of strategic goods to Soviet-bloc countries, we consult and coordinate with fourteen other Free World industrial countries through a Coordinating Committee, known as COCOM. We have never embargoed or opposed the sale of foodstuffs to Soviet bloc countries. Thus, our current sales of wheat to the Soviet Union involved no change in basic policy. And from a traditional Yankee trading viewpoint, we are not unhappy about swapping surplus foodstuffs for gold and hard currency which help to balance our international payments.

Our capacity to influence events and trends within the Communist world is very limited. But it is our policy to do what we can to encourage evolution in the Communist world toward national independence and open societies. We favor more contacts between the peoples behind the Iron Curtain and our own peoples. We should like to see more Soviet citizens visit the United States. We would be glad to join in cooperative enterprises to further mankind's progress against disease, poverty and ignorance. We applaud the interest of the Soviet leadership in improving the lot of the Soviet people.

Thus our policy toward international communism has three objectives:

(1) To prevent the Communists from extending their domain; and to make it increasingly costly, dangerous, and futile for them to try to do so;

(2) To achieve agreements or understandings which reduce the danger of a devastating war;

(3) To encourage evolution within the Communist world to-

ward national independence, peaceful cooperation and open societies.

We believe that we can best promote these objectives by adjusting our policies to the differing behavior of different Communist states — or to the changing behavior of the same state.

When Yugoslavia challenged Stalin's centralized control of Communist affairs in 1948, we gave that country military and economic assistance. Yugoslavia not only defied Stalin but stopped supporting the guerrilla aggression against Greece, reached an agreement with Italy on Trieste, and increased its economic, political and cultural ties with the West. It is not a member of the Warsaw Pact. As a non-aligned state, it has gained influence among the uncommitted nations of the world. Sometimes it agrees with the Soviet Union on particular points of foreign policy, sometimes not. In brief, Yugoslavia is an independent state. Its success in defending its independence made other peoples in Eastern Europe wonder why they could not do likewise. And not least important from our viewpoint, Yugoslavia is not shipping arms to be used against a democratic government in Venezuela, and is not trying to destroy non-Communist governments in South Viet Nam and Laos.

For some years, we have treated Poland somewhat differently from other Soviet bloc states. A good deal of the national autonomy and domestic liberalization which the Poles won in 1956 persists. Most of Polish agriculture remains in private hands; religion is strong; Poland has developed a broad range of relations and exchanges with the West. Poland has historic ties with the West. And its people are the close blood relatives of many citizens of the United States. We apologize to none for our efforts to help the brave people of Poland to preserve their national identity and their own aspirations.

At one time we felt compelled to break diplomatic relations with Bulgaria. Since the ruthless suppression of the Hungarian national revolution in 1956, we have been represented in Budapest not by a regular envoy but by a Chargé. We have never had diplomatic relations with Communist Albania, the most blatantly Stalinist state in Europe.

Thus, for good reasons, we have treated various Soviet bloc states differently and the same state differently at different times. And we shall continue to differentiate our policy according to the conduct of the various Communist states.

Recently Rumania has asserted a more independent attitude and has expanded its trade and other contacts with the West. It has taken steps to improve its relations with the United States. We are responding accordingly.

Hungary has turned to a more permissive policy of national conciliation. We of course welcome any tendencies promising to ease the lot of the Hungarian people. We will do what we can to encourage them.

In Czechoslovakia and Bulgaria there are some signs of movement away from earlier and harsher policies. We are watching these developments with close attention.

F THE RAPACKI PLAN (Warsaw, February 14, 1958)

The Polish Government Memorandum Concerning the
Creation of an Atom-Free Zone in Central Europe

On October 2, 1957, the Government of the Polish People's Republic presented to the General Assembly of the United Nations a proposal concerning the establishment of a denuclearised zone in
Central Europe. The Governments of Czechoslovakia and of the
German Democratic Republic declared their readiness to accede
to that zone.

The Government of the Polish People's Republic proceeded
with the conviction that the establishment of the proposed denuclearised zone could lead to an improvement in the international
atmosphere and facilitate broader discussions on disarmament as
well as the solution of other controversial international issues,
while the continuation of nuclear armaments and making them
universal could only lead to a further solidifying of the division
of Europe into opposing blocs and to a further complication of
the situation, especially in Central Europe.

In December 1957, the Government of the Polish People's Republic renewed their proposal through diplomatic channels.

Considering the wide repercussions which the Polish initiative
has evoked and taking into account the proposition emerging from
the discussion which has developed on this proposal, the Government of the Polish People's Republic hereby present a more detailed elaboration of their proposal, which may facilitate the opening of negotiations and reaching of an agreement on this subject.

I. The proposed zone should include the territory of: Poland,
Czechoslovakia, German Democratic Republic and German Federal Republic. In this territory nuclear weapons would neither be
manufactured nor stockpiled, the equipment and installations designed for their servicing would not be located there, the use of
nuclear weapons against the territory of this zone would be pro-
hibited.

SOURCE: *The Rapacki Plan, Documents* (Warsaw: Department of Information, Polish Press Agency, 1961), pp. 4–6.

II. The contents of the obligations arising from the establish-ment of the denuclearised zone would be based upon the follow-ing premises:

1.The States included in this zone would undertake the obliga-tion not to manufacture, maintain or import for their own use and not to permit the location on their territories of nuclear weapons of any type, as well as not to install on or to admit to their territories of installations and equipment designed for serv-icing nuclear weapons, including missiles-launching equipment.

2. The four Powers (France, United States, Great Britain and U.S.S.R.) would undertake the following obligations:

a) Not to maintain nuclear weapons in the armaments of their forces stationed on the territories of States included in this zone; neither to maintain nor to install on the territories of these States any installations or equipment designed for serv-icing nuclear weapons, including missiles launching equip-ment.

b) Not to transfer in any manner and under any reason what-soever, nuclear weapons or installations and equipment designed for servicing nuclear weapons, to governments or other organs in this area.

3. The Powers which have at their disposal nuclear weapons should undertake the obligation not to use these weapons against the territory of the zone or against any targets situated in this zone.

Thus the Powers would undertake the obligation to respect the status of the zone as an area in which there should be no nuclear weapons and against which nuclear weapons should not be used.

4. Other States, whose forces are stationed on the territory of any state included in the zone, would also undertake the obligation not to maintain nuclear weapons in the armaments of these forces and not to transfer such weapons to Governments or to other organs in this area. Neither will they install equipment or installa-tions designed for the servicing of nuclear weapons, including missiles-launching equipment, on the territories of States in the zone nor will they transfer them to Governments or other organs in this area.

The manner and procedure for the implementation of these ob-ligations could be the subject of detailed mutual stipulations.

III. 1. In order to ensure the effectiveness and the implementa-tion of the obligations contained in part II, para 1–2 and 4, the States concerned would undertake to create a system of broad and effective control in the area of the proposed zone and submit them-selves to its functioning.

The system could comprise ground as well as aerial control. Adequate control posts, with rights and possibilities of action which would ensure the effectiveness of inspection, could also be established.

The details and forms of the implementation of control can be agreed upon on the basis of the experience acquired up to the present time in this field, as well as on the basis of proposals submitted by various States in the course of the disarmament negotiations, in the form and to the extent in which they can be adapted to the area of the zone.

The system of control established for the denuclearised zone could provide useful experiences for the realization of broader disarmament agreement.

2. For the purpose of supervising the implementation of the proposed obligations an adequate control machinery should be established. There could participate in it, for example, representatives appointed (not excluding ad personam appointments) by organs of the North Atlantic Treaty Organization and of the Warsaw Treaty. Nationals or representatives of States, which do not belong to any military grouping in Europe, could also participate in it.

IV. The procedure of the establishment, operation and reporting of the control organs can be the subject of further mutual stipulations.

The most simple form of embodying the obligations of States included in the zone would be the conclusion of an appropriate international convention. To avoid, however, complications, which some States might find in such a solution, it can be arranged that:

1. These obligations be embodied in the form of four unilateral declarations, bearing the character of an international obligation, deposited with a mutually agreed upon depository State;

2. The obligations of Great Powers be embodied in the form of a mutual document or unilateral declarations (as mentioned above in para 1);

3. The obligations of other States, whose armed forces are stationed in the area of the zone, be embodied in the form of unilateral declarations (as mentioned above in para 1).

On the basis of the above proposals the Government of the Polish People's Republic suggest to initiate negotiations for the purpose of a further detailed elaboration of the plan for the establishment of the denuclearised zone, of the documents and guarantees related to it as well as of the means of implementation of the undertaken obligations.

The Government of the Polish People's Republic have reasons to state that acceptance of the proposal concerning the establishment of a denuclearised zone in Central Europe will facilitate the reaching of an agreement relating to an adequate reduction of conventional armaments and of foreign armed forces stationed on the territory of the States included in the zone.

G THE MODIFIED RAPACKI PLAN (Gomulka Plan), February 1964

Memorandum of the Government of the Polish People's Republic on the Freezing of Nuclear and Thermonuclear Armaments in Central Europe

The Government of the Polish People's Republic has already on numerous occasions manifested its consistent desire in the search for solutions aimed at bringing about international detente and disarmament and lent its support to all constructive proposals designed to achieve this end. The reduction of international tension and creating of conditions of security in Central Europe have always been and continue to be matters of particular concern to the Polish Government. This objective can and should be achieved above all by way of arresting the armaments race in this part of the world.

With this in mind the Government of the Polish People's Republic presented some time ago a plan for the creation of a nuclear-free zone in Europe which as is known aroused the interest of numerous states and of world public opinion. In the view of the Polish Government that plan continues to be fully topical.

The Polish Government believes that there are at the present time suitable conditions for undertaking immediate measures the implementation of which could facilitate further steps leading to a detente, to a strengthening of security and to progress in the field of disarmament.

Basing itself on these premises the Government of the Polish People's Republic is submitting a proposal to freeze nuclear and thermonuclear armaments in Central Europe. The implementation of such a proposal would be of particular significance to the security both of Poland and of all countries of this region as well as of the whole of Europe, since, while in no way affecting the existing relation of forces, it would contribute to the arrest of the nuclear armaments race.

SOURCE: Embassy of the Polish People's Republic, Washington. Press release, March 6, 1964.

127

I. The Polish Government proposes that the freezing of nuclear and thermonuclear armaments include in principle the territories of the Polish People's Republic, the Czechoslovak Socialist Republic, the German Democratic Republic and the Federal Republic of Germany, with the respective territorial waters and air space.

The Government of the Polish People's Republic sees the possibility of extending that area through the accession of other European states.

II. The freeze would apply to all kinds of nuclear and thermonuclear charges, irrespective of the means of their employment and delivery.

III. Parties maintaining armed forces in the area of the proposed freeze of armaments would undertake obligations not to produce, not to introduce or import, not to transfer to other parties in the area or to accept from other parties in the area the aforementioned nuclear and thermonuclear weapons.

IV. To ensure the implementation of those obligations an appropriate system of supervision and safeguards should be established.

The supervision over the implementation of the obligation not to produce nuclear and thermonuclear weapons covered by the freeze would be exercised in plants which are or could be used for such production.

To ensure the implementation of other obligations control would be established to be exercised in accordance with an agreed procedure in proper frontier railway, road, waterway junctions, sea and airports.

The supervision and control could be exercised by mixed commissions composed of representatives of the Warsaw Pact and of the North Atlantic Treaty on a parity basis. Those commissions could be enlarged to include also representatives of other states. The composition, structure and procedure of the control organs will be subject of detailed arrangements. Parties whose armed forces are stationed in the area of the armaments freeze and which have at their disposal nuclear and thermonuclear weapons would exchange at periodical meetings of their representatives all information and reports indispensable for the implementation of the obligations with regard to the freezing of nuclear and thermonuclear armaments.

V. Provisions relating to the implementation of the proposal submitted above should be embodied in appropriate documents.

The Government of the Polish People's Republic is ready to enter into discussions and negotiations with the interested parties to reach an agreement on the implementation of these objectives.

The Polish Government will give due attention to all constructive suggestions, which would be in accordance with the objectives of the present proposal and would aim at the freezing of armaments in Central Europe.

The Government of the Polish People's Republic expects a favorable attitude to the proposal submitted hereby.

INDEX

INDEX

133